CHILDREN WHO SEE TOO MUCH

Children Who See Too Much

Lessons from the Child Witness to Violence Project

BETSY MCALISTER GROVES

Beacon Press

BOSTON

Beacon Press
25 Beacon Street
Boston, Massachusetts 02108-2892
www.beacon.org

Beacon Press books
are published under the auspices of
the Unitarian Universalist Association of Congregations.

Printed in the United States of America

14 11 10

This book is printed on acid-free paper that meets the uncoated paper ANSI/NISO specifications for permanence as revised in 1992.

Composition by Wilsted & Taylor Publishing Services

Library of Congress Cataloging-in-Publication Data
Groves, Betsy McAlister.
Children who see too much : lessons from the child witness to violence project / Betsy McAlister Groves.
p. cm.
Includes bibliographical references and index.
ISBN 978-0-8070-3139-1 (pbk.)
1. Children and violence. I. Title.
HQ784.V55 G76 2002
303.6'083—dc21

2001004409

CONTENTS

REFLECTIONS ON THE EVENTS OF SEPTEMBER 11, 2001

On September 11, as this book was in the final stages of production, the nation's basic conceptions of safety and security were forever changed as we helplessly watched a series of attacks centered in New York City and Washington, D.C., that left more than three thousand people dead, obliterated fourteen acres of lower Manhattan, resulted in the loss of thousands of jobs, and left countless heroic helpers numb with trauma. Collectively terrified, we don't know what will happen next; we don't know who or what the enemy is; we look suspiciously at strangers; we stock up on antibiotics to protect ourselves against the invisible.

In chapter 2 of this book, I describe in some detail how exposure to violence transforms children's views of the world and changes their basic ability to trust that they can be safe. I make the point that one does not have to be a direct victim of violence to experience this fundamental change in outlook on the world. Experts who write about children and trauma describe that children develop "pervasive pessimism" or a "sense of foreshortened future" and that this sense of doom stays with them for a long time. It strikes me that these terms are now applicable to all of us. The notion of children seeing too much has become the reality of a country seeing too much and enduring too much loss. This reality we now share with millions in a world too often overwhelmed by violence.

We as adults can get our minds around community violence or domestic violence, and we can think of ways to help children. But can we even know how to talk about this national horror? How can we help children if we are paralyzed with our realization of the fragility of life and peace?

The Child Witness to Violence Project, along with mental health agencies throughout the country, received many calls for assistance in the weeks following September 11. The calls largely focused on questions about how to talk with children about what had happened and how to help children feel less scared. Parents told us that their children were afraid to go to school and didn't want their parents to go to work. One child was worried because his school was on the third floor of a building. To this child, the building was like a skyscraper. A kindergarten teacher in New York City said that her children wouldn't lie down at rest time without their shoes on because of their fear that they might have to flee the building at a moment's notice. One child, whose father flies frequently for business, drew a picture of her father as Superman and gave it to him as he left for work. She made no comment about the picture, but her wish was apparent. Older children wondered why others hated this country so much or whether we were going to war. In response to the many requests for information, we developed guidelines for parents of young children to give them support in talking with their children. (They are included in the appendix to this book.) Even as we put the words on paper, we struggled with the large questions: "How do we understand such evil in the world?" "Why would anyone hate a country enough to unleash such terror?" "How can buildings the size and strength of the World Trade Center be totally destroyed?" "In the continuing atmosphere of fear and uncertainty, how can anyone feel safe?" These are the hard questions that we now live with.

In the near future, a major task for this country will be to restore some equilibrium, both psychologically and economically. We will work to stay calm and to protect our children. As a nation, we will continue to struggle with rage and the impulse for violent retribution. We will face with heavy hearts the prospects of an expanded or prolonged cycle of violence and terror. In the midst of our anguish, however, we will continue to see resilience and spirit. We will draw together as families and communities and seek strength in companionship. We will become ever more aware of the interdependency of all the world's nations. One of the central messages of this book is that relationships are a powerful tool in helping children heal from the trauma of violence. My hope is that a spirit of human connection and interdependence will guide the way to our continued recovery.

Betsy McAlister Groves
October 11, 2001

CHILDREN WHO SEE TOO MUCH

INTRODUCTION

Several weeks after we opened the doors of the Child Witness to Violence Project at Boston Medical Center, we got a distraught call from the grandmother of a two-and-a-half-year-old boy. This child had been with his mother when she was fatally shot in her home. The grandmother told us that her grandson had not slept for many nights, that he woke screaming, and that on several nights he had been found in his room on his hands and knees, trying to wipe something off the floor. She was quite upset and wondered if she should bring her grandson in for an evaluation. She had initially consulted the boy's pediatrician, who cautioned against it, saying that because the boy was so young, he most likely would not remember what had happened. We advised the grandmother to bring the boy in. In a play session with this child, he told me that his mom "was on the floor" and that she "didn't talk." He subsequently spoke about a man with a gun. He was extremely fearful of loud noises, and his grandmother said that once when he saw a blue car, he had said, "The man with the gun is in there." The pediatrician had assumed that the boy's age would protect him from the effects of this traumatic experience. She was wrong. As we at Boston Medical Center gained experience in this area, we saw the myth of young age as a protection from the effects of violence disproved over and over again.

Since 1992, the Child Witness to Violence Project has offered counseling services to children and families by a staff of therapists and child development specialists. This program has been nationally recognized as unique and innovative, making a significant contribution to the understanding of how exposure to violence affects young children. Each staff member has training in treating traumatized children and blends this training with a solid knowledge of early child development. The program is part of the Department of Pediatrics at Boston Medical Center and embodies the hospital's recognition that children's health encompasses psychological and social well-being as well as physical health. Referrals come from a wide range of sources, reflecting the many places that children are seen. Police, physicians, teachers, attorneys, clergy, social workers, and day care providers make referrals. We see children from all backgrounds because violence knows no class, ethnic, racial, or geographic boundaries.

This book grew out of my work with the Project. It examines what happens when young children witness violence in their communities and homes. While the names and certain identifying details of the children and families presented in this book have been changed to protect their confidentiality, their stories are real. They speak strongly about the ways in which exposure to violence changes the landscape of childhood forever. Woven throughout the narrative of the stories is the strong and healing presence of parents, caregivers, teachers, and other adults. The message of these stories has two parts. First, many children in this country are growing up in a sea of violence and violent images, and it is destroying their abilities to be hopeful and trusting of adults. The second message is that we as adults have enormous capacity to help these children.

This book is for anyone who cares about young children. Many parents, teachers, health providers, police officers, counselors, and day care providers are all too familiar with stories like these and their messages. I offer a special invitation to those who do not work directly with children and who would not have the opportunity to hear from children about how violence affects their lives. If our future rests with the children of this nation, then we must all be concerned about and invested in their safe growth and development. This books invites each of you to bear witness to the lives of many children growing up in the United States today. It is a call to action to begin the process of creating a safer society for our children.

CHAPTER I

Violence in the Lives of Young Children

In 1990, when my two daughters were old enough for preschool, I returned to full-time work as the clinical coordinator at the Family Development Center, a day care center located on the premises of Boston City Hospital (later known as Boston Medical Center). This job entailed direct counseling with children and their parents, as well as coordinating other special services the families needed. The day care center, like the hospital, was well known for providing services to children and families struggling with poverty, inadequate housing, or addictions. The children, even at preschool age, had many vulnerabilities. Some had been neglected or abused as infants; others had significant eating problems and were not growing adequately. Some had been born to drug-involved mothers. At the Family Development Center, however, every child was welcomed into a small classroom with ample individual attention from the teacher. These children also received medical and mental health evaluations and other specialized services if needed. Their parents were involved in the program through parenting groups and individual counseling.

I had been at the center for about six months when two things occurred that began to change the way I thought about risks to young children. The first incident took place as the children were being bused home from school at the end of the day. As the van, filled with preschoolers and their teacher aide, made its way through the neighborhoods of Boston, the driver was forced to stop suddenly to avoid hitting a man who staggered in front of the van. The man was bleeding profusely and was being pursued by another man wielding a knife. The victim collapsed in front of the van, and the assailant disappeared. The aide turned to look at the children. They were wide eyed and silent, staring at the man who lay in a pool of blood. The police arrived immediately; the victim was removed, and the van continued its route, dropping children off at their homes. The aide reassured the children that they would be OK. There was little other conversation in the van.

When the aide, Barbara, returned to school, our weekly staff meeting was in progress. Very upset, she told us what had happened on the van. As we listened to her story, we began to think about how to help the children. Our first step was to call each parent to let him or her know what the children had seen. Then we began to plan for the next day. We wondered how children this age would understand what they had seen. At that time, there wasn't much published research on the effects on young children of witnessing violence, much less training or resource centers that could teach us. Would it make an impression on them? How does a three-year-old think about seeing a man covered with blood? What does a five-year-old understand about seeing another man run across the street with a knife? How do young children make sense of such frightening events? What in their previous life experience might help or hinder their abilities to cope with the fear they might feel? The other set of questions we struggled with was how we, as adult caregivers, could help these children understand and cope. What words should we use? What kind of explanation should we give them? Should we bring the incident up immediately tomorrow morning, or should we wait until they mentioned it? We were unsure how best to help the children, partly because we were horrified and partly, perhaps, because we felt guilty that as their caregivers we had not been able to protect them from seeing what they had seen. We finally formulated a strategy for the next day. We decided to wait until one of the children brought up the incident before we talked about it with them. This decision, we felt, would ensure that we would respond to the children's perspectives, rather than making adult assumptions about what they knew or understood.

I went home that night to my husband and two daughters. I was troubled by this incident and began to think about how my own daughters would react if they saw something similar. I also began to think about the striking differences in the life experiences of my daughters compared to those of the children I worked with at the Family Development Center. My family, with adequate resources, is fortunate to live in a safe neighborhood. I didn't believe that my children had ever seen anything frightening or dangerous in our community. Their experience stood in stark contrast to the experiences of the children at the center. Many of these children lived in chronically dangerous environments. The dangers existed both within their homes and in the community, as families struggled with violence, crime, gangs, and poverty. My personal variation of guilt centered on my belief that children's safety should be a basic right, not a privilege that comes with social class or education. I thought about the conversations I had had with parents in the center. These parents had children the same ages as my children, and their aspirations for their children were the same as mine. We all wanted our children to be able to learn in school, to succeed in their lives, and to grow up safely. Yet, for many of these parents, these goals would not likely be attained.

The children arrived at school the next day and we waited all morning to hear any references to the incident. There were none. It seemed as though nothing had happened. Finally, one of the teachers decided to bring up the issue in circle time. She told the children that Barbara had told her about what had happened on the van. There was a brief silence, and then the children began to talk. They had many questions: What happened to the man who was lying on the street? How much blood is inside our bodies? Was that man at our hospital? Was he dead? Why did the bad man stab him? Could the doctors sew him up? Where was the bad man? Had the police arrested him? Could he break out of jail? In answer to this last question, one little boy began to tell a long story about a TV program that showed how easy it was to get out of jail. The children could not stop talking about what they had seen. They also talked about similar events, some of which they had seen on television, some of which were real-life concerns. One girl spoke of seeing a man shot in her apartment building, an experience we had never heard from her before.

As the staff reviewed this extraordinary group discussion, we began to formulate answers to some of our original questions. Yes, this incident had made a big impression on the children. Their questions and perceptions of the event were filtered through the lens of their cognitive and psychological stages of development. Two main themes emerged from our discussion. The first theme had to do with the vulnerability of the human body. Many questions centered on what happens to the body when it is injured. These questions were asked in typical preschool fashion, sometimes catching the adults off guard. However, they reflected the fear of many children that their bodies might be vulnerable in the same way. What we began to hear were the deeper fears of destruction and death: "If this could happen to an adult, it could happen to me, too. I am not safe."

The second theme the children elaborated on was the power of the "bad man," as they called him. Their questions about the motives for the stabbing reflected the beginnings of moral development and the quest to understand consequences of behavior. One little girl wondered if the victim had done something wrong. It seemed as though she were questioning if this were how you were punished if you were really bad. Linked to this worry was the equally strong fear that the assailant was so powerful that no jail could hold him. Again, the children were telling us about their profound fear and vulnerability. Once a child has seen something as scary as this incident, perhaps he or she cannot feel safe again.

The staff learned valuable lessons from this exchange with the children. Over the years, as we have heard similar stories from hundreds of young children, these themes of basic vulnerability, lack of safety, and chronic fear have been sounded over and over again. We now know that when young children witness an extremely scary event, their outlook on the world and on their place in it changes dramatically, and that this shift in worldview affects their behavior in many spheres.

The other lesson we learned was that we as adults must give children permission to talk about violence in their lives. In retrospect, we understood that our reluctance to bring up the issue with the children was in fact a conspiracy of silence. We colluded with the children in avoiding talking about the issue that was so obviously on everyone's mind. When the teacher mentioned the incident, the children finally understood that they could talk about it. We have seen this phenomenon many times in our work with children. If we as adults do not talk about a frightening event, children may believe that it is too scary for the adults or that the subject is somehow taboo. This experience also gave us powerful information about how to help children.

The second incident that focused my interest on the risks to children exposed to violence occurred about one month later. It was a much more overwhelming event involving the murder of the mother of two of the center's children.

Most of the staff found out about the murder from the television news. The media reported that a woman had been fatally shot in her home during a robbery attempt. Her husband, in attempting to protect his wife, had also been shot, but his injuries were not life threatening. The reporter went on to say that their children had been home during the incident but were unharmed.

We have grown accustomed to nightly lead stories about murder, mayhem, or disaster. In fact, they are covered with such repetition that one becomes numb to their meaning: another faceless victim of crime, another number, another incident that labels a particular neighborhood as dangerous. We barely listen. This murder victim, however, was neither faceless nor nameless. This was Tram, mother of Hoang, age four, and Lan, age five. I had made a visit to the house two weeks before. Tram had greeted me warmly. She was a slight woman with a pretty smile. I knew that she and her husband had escaped from Cambodia some ten years before and had spent years in Thailand at a refugee camp. They had lost several family members in the war and had suffered enormously in the refugee camps. As Tram greeted me graciously, I remember wondering about the unspeakable horrors she must have endured before coming to this country. Although she spoke little English, we were able to talk about her six children and how they were doing at the school. Hoang and Lan were the youngest. All the children slept in the same room, a large room with mattresses. In her living room, where we sat, were a sofa, a television, and a small table. Otherwise the house was bare.

The memories of this visit washed over me as I heard the news. My first reaction was one of rage. How could this woman, who had no possessions, be killed in a robbery? My next reaction was overwhelming sadness. This couple had endured years of trauma in refugee camps and had arrived in this country assuming that they were now safe. For them, as with so many immigrant families, the United States held promises of freedom, safety, and relative affluence. And yet this woman had been brutally murdered.

At the hastily called staff meeting the next day, we shared many memories of Tram's family. As a staff, we were devastated. We were paralyzed in thinking about how to support the other children at the center because we ourselves felt such grief and anger. One teacher put it directly by saying, "How can I support my kids when I can't deal with this? What am I supposed to say to the children? They all know about it."

Once again, we had to devise a plan for responding to children's questions and fears. Heeding the lessons from the first experience, we structured circle meetings for the children at the beginning of the day. Some of the children knew about the murder; others did not. We began the meeting by saying to the children that we had very sad news to share with them. We told them that Hoang and Lan's mother had died. We waited for the first question, "How did she die?" One boy said, "She got shot. I saw it on the news." The teacher affirmed the story and asked what other children knew. Encouraging the children to talk, she then clarified inaccurate information. Once again, the children responded in ways that were consistent with their development. They voiced fear about the safety of their families. One child talked about the fact that his mother had been attacked. And they asked about the robbers. Where were they? Were the police looking for them? The fact that they had not been apprehended worried the children.

Because this traumatic event hit so close to home for students and staff, its aftermath was evident for weeks. Hoang and Lan came back to school. A couple of days after they returned, the murder suspects were arrested. Once again, there was media coverage with a front-page picture of the three suspects. In my therapy session with Hoang, he asked if I had seen the picture. I indicated that I had and that I had a copy of the newspaper with me. Together we looked at the picture. Hoang remembered that the men were wearing masks during the robbery. He asked if we could take the picture to show his classmates. I hesitated, unsure of what disruption this might cause in the classroom. However, Hoang was so insistent that his friends see the picture that I assented, and we went down the hall to the classroom. The teacher handled this situation smoothly. She announced that Hoang had a picture he wanted to share with the class. She reminded the class about what had happened to Hoang's mother. Hoang showed the picture to his friends, telling them, "These are the men who killed my mom," and there was great interest in the picture. The children gathered around to see the newspaper. Together, the teacher and I responded to questions and comments. The children wanted to know about jail and how long the men would be there. They also wanted to know about the motive. Why had they shot Hoang's mother? Hoang looked at his teacher, who responded, "We don't know why they shot your mother. They were really mixed up and what they did was very bad." One of the children wanted to draw a picture of a jail. This became the art project for the day.

Once again, the teacher and I wondered about whether we were handling this situation the right way. There seemed to be no script for how we should proceed. Should we have let Hoang bring his picture to the classroom? Was this too upsetting for the children? What did it mean to the children to have an art lesson focus on drawing jails? We were also unsure about the reaction of the children's parents, who may not have wanted this event to be discussed in the classroom.

As we coped during the next several months in the center, we came to have more confidence in the way we had handled this terrible trauma for Hoang. He continued to talk about what he had seen. He spoke of the event frequently, both in the classroom and in his therapy sessions with me. It was as though he was trying to make sense of the insanity and horror by going over it again and again. He used his classmates, his teacher, and his therapist as helpers in this endeavor. The frequent references to the event did not seem to have an adverse impact on the classroom or on the children's behavior at home. In fact, it may have helped reassure the other kids to know that they could talk about it. They were supported and guided by an extraordinarily sensitive and skilled teacher who used her close relationships with the children to judge what could be talked about, and when.

Lan, in another classroom, seemed to be assimilating her loss in a different and perhaps more worrisome way. She avoided talking about the murder in class or in therapy. Instead, she withdrew. She rarely played or participated in group activities. The contrast in styles of coping was notable and made us wonder about why children react to events so differently. Did she experience the loss differently? Was the difference because of age? Was it a question of gender, individual style, or temperament? What were the implications of coping style for longer-term adjustment? We could not answer these questions.

Together, these two incidents at the Family Development Center focused the staff on the ripple effect that violent events have for communities and society. We began to see that there are, in fact, many victims for each act of aggression, harm, or violence that is committed. The man who was stabbed on the street that day was surely a victim, but so too were the children in the van. While Hoang and Lan struggled with the horror of losing their mother, so too did their classmates, who now knew that moms and dads are vulnerable to bullets and can die. We began to worry that this awareness would change children's lives forever, and that each time they were witness to harm, violence, and injury, their basic trust in the world as a safe and predictable place would be eroded.

THE BEGINNING OF THE CHILD WITNESS TO VIOLENCE PROJECT

At our hospital, we found that the worry about children's exposure to violence was not exclusive to child care providers. Discussion with our pediatric colleagues at Boston Medical Center revealed that they, too, heard many stories about violence in young children's lives. Doctors saw children for well-child visits, and heard from mothers about not being able to take their children to the park because the neighborhood was unsafe. Also, children told their doctors that they heard gunshots at night. Together, we decided to take a broader look at the problem. We knew that children in the Family Development Center were seeing a lot of violence. We knew that the homicide rates in Boston had steadily escalated. Information was also emerging from other studies about elementary schoolchildren's exposure to violence. For instance, a study conducted in a New Orleans neighborhood in the early 1990s found that 90 percent of the children had witnessed violence, and 40 percent had seen a dead body.[1] In Los Angeles, it was estimated that children witnessed 10 to 20 percent of homicides in that city.[2] But what about preschoolers' exposure to violence? Does age somehow protect them from this risk?

To obtain more accurate information about the rate of very young children's exposure to violence, we designed a small study of families with children under age six who used the pediatric services at Boston Medical Center.[3] The focus of this study was a questionnaire given to mothers in the waiting room of the clinic. Participation in the study was optional: If mothers agreed to be part of the study, they were interviewed by a trained interviewer and answered various questions about their children's exposure to violence. Participants were recruited directly from the waiting room. In all, 115 mothers were interviewed. All had at least one child under age six.

The findings were sobering. Forty-seven percent of the mothers reported that their child had heard gunshots. Ninety-four percent of these mothers reported more than one episode. Ten percent of the children had directly witnessed a knifing or a shooting; nearly twice that number had witnessed an episode of hitting, kicking, or shoving. The average age of the child in this study was 2.7 years. When we asked the mothers whose children had been exposed to violence about the consequences of that exposure, we found that parents most frequently worried that their children would become habituated to the violence and think that violence was the norm. They also worried about how violence would limit their children's growth and freedom.

This study proved to be a wake-up call about young children's exposure to violence.[4] Our findings indicated that young children were being exposed to violence with alarming frequency. From the data generated from this study, we were able to secure funding for the Child Witness to Violence Project.

The Project opened its doors in 1992. From the beginning, it has served young children ages eight and under. Although we knew that exposure to violence was harmful to children of all ages, we felt strongly about focusing our resources on young children. We believed that there were fewer resources for them, in part because there was less recognition that they were affected. Referrals have come from police, physicians, teachers, attorneys, and day care providers. Agencies such as children's protective services, Head Start, and battered women's shelters also identify children needing help. Since our program has become better known, parents are calling on their own to ask about services. Sometimes a parent isn't sure whether the child should be seen. "My child has seen her father and me fighting. The other night things got out of hand. He hit me. I'm worried about my child." In response to a query like this, we encourage the parent to come in without the child, so that we can discuss the concerns in more depth and then decide together whether the child should be evaluated.

THE FIRST REFERRAL

Marlene Williams had the dubious distinction of being Boston's first homicide of 1992. She died in her home around lunchtime on January 8, the victim of a shooting. I did not know Marlene in life, but I will never forget her son, Daquan, age four years, two months, partially because he was the first referral to the Child Witness to Violence Project and partly because of the horror of his story. Before seeing him, I received basic information from the emergency department's social worker. Daquan had been with his mother at the time of her death, which the police established had happened between nine and ten in the morning. A neighbor discovered Daquan and his mother's body in the early afternoon. Daquan was upstairs sleeping at the time. From what Daquan told the police, they believed it was possible that he had witnessed the murder; however, he seemed confused, and a speech impediment did not help his ability to communicate. He and his mother were brought to Boston City Hospital. There was a suspect, the current boyfriend of Daquan's mother. However, there was no firm evidence of his guilt.

I was also given the newspaper account of the murder: "A 36-year-old mother of three became Boston's first homicide victim of the year when she was shot in her home yesterday and died on the way to Boston City Hospital. One neighbor said that she had been shot several times in the chest. The victim was found lying on her living room floor around 12:15. . . . Her four-year-old son, Daquan, was in the house at the time of the shooting, but was not hurt."[5] The article went on to say that Daquan's two teenage sisters learned of the shooting when they got off the bus from school and saw yellow police tape around their house.

I remember feeling nervous about my first meeting with Daquan. I thought my anxiety was somewhat ironic, given the fact that he was a four-year-old boy and I was a clinician with many years' experience as a therapist. My nervousness centered on how I would begin to talk to him about the violent death of his mother. I rehearsed statements or questions in my head, trying to think about a gentle, nonintrusive way of bringing up the subject.

I thought about which activities might be most appropriate for a child this age. I had drawing materials, a doctor's kit, cars, and a dollhouse available.

Daquan was to be brought to the hospital by a family friend. According to this friend, he seemed to be in a daze. He was confused about where his mother was, he had trouble sleeping, and he refused to talk about what had happened. Detectives had interviewed him a short time after the murder, but his story was still garbled.

I went to the waiting room to greet Daquan. Without a moment's hesitation, he stood up and announced loudly that his mother had been shot. He then reenacted the way she fell to the floor, by saying, "She fell down . . . just like this." In an instant, we had begun our therapeutic relationship. My initial worry about how to help him begin to talk about the trauma was groundless. He could not wait to talk about it. What I should have worried about was how to help him stop talking and thinking about it. I learned that this event was utterly overwhelming to him and that it pervaded every aspect of his being. I also understood that my anxiety about what words to use was a foil for my helplessness and horror about this murder. In a sense, I was speechless because there are no words that are adequate in such situations. I discovered that no amount of clinical experience could protect me from the horror of this event and from the realization of what human beings can do to one another.

For the next six months, Daquan and I were immersed in the horror of what had happened. For the first several sessions, Daquan said little about the murder other than that his mother had been shot and she was on the floor. He also told me about her funeral: "Mommy died and she is in a box. Then she went to heaven. I don't want to go there." It seemed that he had a series of disconnected images of his mother. She was lying on the floor; she was in a box. I believed he was struggling to figure out where she was. It was as though the figures he saw on the floor and in the box could not be his mother. Other than making these few utterances, Daquan played with toys. He liked playing with cars and trucks, a typical four-year-old boy's activity. However, Daquan's particular game with them perhaps spoke to the trauma he had suffered. He played the same game each week: The truck was filled with people; he drove it along the side of the table, veering closer and closer to the edge, until the truck with its occupants fell to the floor. Then Daquan announced, "They are all dead now." He repeated this sequence countless times. It was a singular pursuit. He did not involve me in the play and seemed oblivious to my comments.

When Daquan came in for the fifth session, he asked if we could draw pictures. After I produced the drawing material, he said, once again, " My mommy got shot." I asked him if he would like to draw a picture about that. He replied that he could not draw and asked if I could. He directed me. "Draw a lady on the floor." He then took a red crayon and drew all over her. I asked if that was blood. He said, "Yes." He then told me more. He told me that a man had shot her and that he had said some bad words. I asked if he knew the man. He did not answer. He told me that the man was wearing a blue shirt and that he talked loudly. He heard a big noise and his mom fell down. He then told me that he had gone upstairs to sleep in his bedroom. I now understood that this event was so overwhelming to Daquan that he had withdrawn to the world of sleep. Daquan grew very quiet and continued to look at the picture. He reached out to touch it and ran his fingers over the drawing of his mother. It was as though he were trying to touch her. I believed that by telling the story and creating a visual image of what happened, Daquan was beginning to understand that his mother was not coming back. It was a profoundly sad moment.

In the next session, Daquan again told the story of what had happened to his mother. As we were sitting at the small table together, playing with Play-Doh, he suddenly asked, "Is your mother dead?" The question caught me by surprise. It slipped past the guard of benign neutrality that therapists are trained to use in clinical work. It went straight to my heart, and I replied, "Yes, she is dead."

"Did she get shot?" "No," I said. "She got very sick and died in a hospital."

"Did she die in this hospital?" he asked. "No," I replied.

"Do you miss your mommy?" he asked. "Yes," I replied.

"I miss my mommy too," he added.

I told him that it was so sad when a mother dies because you miss her and you want to see her again. He nodded. This exchange was extraordinary. I realized that the difference in our ages, races, cultures, and life experiences was irrelevant. For that moment, we were two human beings, sitting in a room together, both of whom had lost our first and primary caregiver forever. As the months went on, Daquan played out his version of his mother's death countless times. He focused on different aspects of the events. He played out elements of what the paramedics did in their attempt to save her. On some occasions, he played the role of the murderer. It seemed as though this play was Daquan's attempt to understand the trauma from as many perspectives as possible. Gradually, it gave way to other activities in the therapy sessions. Daquan began to play basketball, using a Nerf ball and the wastebasket. He delighted in showing me his skills of jumping and twirling in my small office. He confided in me that he wanted to be Scotty Pippin when he grew up. I was grateful he had a vision for growing up.

Meanwhile, outside the therapy office, many people had become involved in Daquan's life. He was now in school with a loving and consistent kindergarten teacher. We discovered that Daquan had not previously had any preschool experience and had limited opportunities to socialize with other children. He was also behind in school-readiness skills. He did not know his colors, he could not use scissors, he had a short attention span, and his language problems were an obstacle to clear communication. The teacher mobilized services within the school to address these needs. Daquan was a sociable child who quickly adapted to school.

A family friend adopted Daquan. His older sister moved out on her own. The younger sister went to live with her father. Daquan saw his sisters frequently. However, their departure from his daily life represented another loss for him.

The murderer was tried and served time. I stopped seeing Daquan after seven months of therapy. His adoptive mother was taking him to Alabama for the summer. We agreed to stay in touch and that Daquan could come to see me any time his family thought it necessary.

The next time I heard from Daquan was just after Martin Luther King Jr. Day the following year. His teacher called to ask for a consultation. She reported that Daquan had become very upset during the school assembly for Martin Luther King. As the speaker began to talk about the fact that King was shot by an assassin, Daquan ran out of the auditorium and hid in a closet in his classroom. When the astonished teacher pulled him out, she found him shaking and saying, "My mommy got shot; my mommy got shot." It became clear that the reference to King's assassination had triggered a flood of disturbing memories for Daquan. He came back to see me for several sessions. After that, I did not see Daquan again.

Daquan's case is unusual for its magnitude of horror and loss. His experience became a symbol for the most unthinkable experiences that children must contend with. We have seen hundreds of children since Daquan first came to us. Fortunately, few children have endured what he experienced.

Our referrals have included children who fled from war-related violence in other countries, children who saw violence on the streets, and children whose war zones are in their own homes. We have seen children who witnessed suicides and those who were in fires. The common bond for these children is that they are the bystanders to horrifying and dangerous acts, and that their world has been forever changed. However, just as we have learned about how children are changed by these events, we have also learned about what helps them withstand the horror and what resources children have to help them in the face of great fear. The subsequent chapters of this book will tell the story, both of what happens to young children as a result of being exposed to overwhelmingly frightening events and also of what we as adults can do to help them.

CHILDREN GROWING UP IN A CULTURE OF VIOLENCE

When I speak to community groups about the topic of children's exposure to violence, I can count on several questions being raised. These questions invariably have to do with exactly what we mean by violence and exposure to violence. These terms are broad and can encompass a wide range of circumstances. Our working definition of a violent event is an action initiated by a human being that makes a child feel threatened, unsafe, or that results in harm to another person. This definition underscores the fact that these actions are of human design and that the child perceives the action as dangerous or harmful. There are, of course, many events that children perceive as dangerous, including natural disasters, accidents, serious illness, and fires. In fact, research exists that focuses on how children cope with all these traumatic events. One of the most consistent findings from this research, however, is that traumatic events initiated by humans carry more psychological risks than do natural disasters. The fact that humans carry out the violence seems to add an extra element of terror for children.

Another important aspect of this definition of violence is that a child's perception of danger changes with age. What seems dangerous to a three-year-old may not seem dangerous to a seven-year-old. Certain elements of a frightening event may be particularly scary to young children but would not affect us as adults. For example, I saw a three-year-old child in our program whose parents fought constantly. Sometimes the fights ended with her father pushing or shoving the mother. When I asked the child to tell me what happened when her mom and dad had a fight, she replied that the balloons popped. I did not understand this response so I asked her to tell me about the balloons. She again told me that the balloons popped and she demonstrated how loud this noise was. I asked her mother about the balloons. Although initially perplexed by this story, the mother suddenly remembered that one of their louder arguments had occurred on the child's birthday and that as they were yelling, a birthday balloon had popped in the next room. She recalled that her daughter started to cry. We then understood that this little girl was most frightened by the sudden, loud noise that she now associated with her parents' fighting. This would not have been the reaction or the understanding of a seven-year-old bystander to these same fights.

We have also learned that the response of young children to a traumatic event depends partly on the response of their caregiver. If a parent is terrified or hysterical, this response will carry more power than the specifics of the scary event. Children are generally adept at reading cues from their parents. For very young children, the cues from parents are particularly influential because they are unlikely to understand cognitively what happened. They "understand" instead that their mother is terrified or that their father is rageful.

Another ambiguous aspect of this working definition of violence is the concept of "exposure." What do we mean by exposure to violence? Of course, it includes being the direct victim of violence. It also includes seeing or hearing violence, or even knowing of its aftermath. The child who sees his mother with facial bruises that were inflicted by her husband is a witness to the violence even if he was not present at the actual fight.

In our work with families, it is not uncommon to be told by parents that their children are not aware of the violence, particularly if we are discussing incidents of violence in the home. Mothers say, "We had a huge fight last night, but the kids were asleep and didn't hear it." When we talk to the children separately from their parents, we discover that they were well aware of the fight. However, because none of the adults talked about it the next day, the children believed that this was not a subject they could discuss with their parents. One particularly memorable instance of this tendency to deny or minimize what children are aware of came with the report of a police officer who referred three children to our project. The officer had responded to a 911 call placed by a concerned person who had heard screams and loud thuds from his upstairs neighbors. When the police arrived, they found the mother, semiconscious, lying on the bed. She had red marks on her neck and bruises on her upper body. The father was preparing to flee. The room was shattered, with furniture lying around, clothing all over the floor, drawers dumped out. The police officer arrested the father and administered first aid to the woman. He then discovered that her three children were in the living room watching TV. In the words of the officer's report, the children "were unhurt and seemed unaware of what had happened." To me, the officer added, "I don't know about these kids. They didn't seem to care what happened. I don't see how they could just sit there and watch TV while their mother was almost killed." The officer seemed to be both perplexed and finding fault with the children.

When we interviewed the children, we heard a very different story. The children were keenly aware of what had happened. They were both terrified and immobilized, using television as their only means of retreating from the horror. The oldest child, a boy of nine, told me that he had gone down the hall twice to see what was going on. Both times he had stopped outside the closed door of the bedroom, struggling with the choice to enter and try to protect his mother. As he recounted this dilemma, he began to cry. He explained to me that there was a strict rule in his house about not entering bedrooms if the door was closed. He said he was scared to go in because of what might happen to him if he broke this rule. Given the power and rage of his father, I could well understand why he was afraid. My heart went out to this child who had struggled with the unthinkable choice of preserving his own safety or attempting to protect his mother. What also became clear was that the officer's appraisal of these children as callous and uncaring was wrong. They responded in the only way that made sense to them in the face of such terror. They attempted to block it out of their consciousness. This defense was costly, however, because it left them with considerable guilt at having abandoned their mother in her time of need.

THE KINDS OF VIOLENCE TO WHICH CHILDREN ARE EXPOSED

Another question we frequently field is about the kinds of violence children are exposed to and the relative harmfulness of different forms of violence. In our training, we delineate three levels of exposure to violence: exposure to media violence, community violence, and violence in the home. This book focuses on children's exposure to real-life violence. However, no book about children who witness violence can begin without a consideration of the many ways children take in cultural messages about the use of violence. Nor can we talk about helping children who have witnessed real-life violence without appreciating that they (and we) live in a culture of violence.

It can be argued that violence and aggression are an inherent part of human nature and social groups. Violence as expressed in public art or literature has been traced back to the cave drawings of early times.[6] Images of torture abound in Christian art and the activity of Roman civilization. Long and brutal wars, public beheadings, and murders were commonplace throughout history. The more recent writings of sociobiologists and animal behaviorists have considered the evolutionary function of violent behavior, particularly violence in males.[7]

However, when one compares developed nations, American society is more violent than most others, when we consider a range of indicators, from homicides, to gun ownership, to violence in the media. Violence is a hallmark of American culture and society. The international image of the United States includes the Columbine shooting, the Oklahoma City bombing, a culture whose heroes include Arnold Schwarzenegger and Sylvester Stallone, and a society whose children know how and where to get guns.

The United States has one of the highest homicide rates in the world. The homicide rate for young men is seventy-three times greater than the rate in similar industrialized nations. The proliferation of guns and other lethal weapons is directly linked to the increased homicide rates among children, as well as to the numbers of violent incidents that children witness. Each day, ten children in the United States are murdered by gunfire, approximately one every two-and-a-half hours. Homicide is the third leading cause of death among all children between the ages of five and fourteen and the leading cause for black youth.[8] As this book discusses the impact of violence on families and young children, it is important to consider the culture in which these families and individuals are embedded.

The social history of the United States emphasizes traditions of individual rights and individualism over the collective good. This philosophical stance underlies the tolerance of violence against women and corporal punishment in families. Historically, these individual rights dictated that a man was the ruler of his household and that matters of family discipline were not the business of government or the courts. Before the late 1800s, children had few rights separate from the family. In fact, agencies to protect the rights of animals were established before agencies to protect children. It wasn't until the 1960s that state agencies with specific legal mandates to protect children from familial abuse and neglect were created. This historical tradition of the supremacy of individual rights also contributes to this country's inability to regulate gun ownership and possession. It is within this culture that families raise children.

Exposure to Media Violence

Because television violence is the most common form of children's exposure, it makes sense to begin with a review of how TV affects children. Ninety-nine percent of American households have at least one television.[9] There is virtually no child (or adult for that matter) who is unaffected by the power of the media.

The development and proliferation of television has revolutionized this society in a relatively short period of time. Fifty years ago, only a small percentage of households could afford a television. These televisions had small screens and produced black-and-white pictures. Networks were able to broadcast programs for only two or three hours in the evening. Now the average preschooler watches three or four hours of television daily. This preschooler watches these programs on a large color screen using a remote control device to choose from dozens of channels.

Television has profoundly changed the way young children receive messages about the outside world. Before the advent of television, parents could decide what to tell children about news from the outside world and when to tell them; they could monitor what was read to children or what children saw. However, with the advent of television, parents' abilities to control these influences from the larger culture have greatly diminished. Some social scientists contend that television has destroyed the boundaries between adult knowledge and child knowledge.[10] Because parents cannot anticipate what will appear next on television, they are less able to protect children from inappropriate or frightening information. A powerful example of the limits of parents' abilities was the *Challenger* disaster, when the manned spacecraft exploded shortly after liftoff in 1986, killing all the astronauts aboard. Because a schoolteacher was aboard the craft, millions of schoolchildren across the country watched the liftoff. Schools had been preparing for days for this event, organizing lessons about this space flight. What was intended to be a science lesson, however, became a horrifying trauma, as students helplessly watched the *Challenger* explode in midair. There was no way that teachers could have anticipated or protected the children from seeing this disaster.

In the last fifty years, the amount of violence in this country has increased exponentially. Researchers point out the parallels between this increase in violence and the proliferation of televisions.[11] In 1951 the U.S. population was 150 million. That year, the national number of homicides was 6,280. In 1980, thirty years later, the population had increased 47 percent, to 220 million. Homicides had increased to 23,000, a 400 percent increase. This rise in violent crime is the result of a complex set of social factors; it would be simplistic, of course, to attribute this rise primarily to television's influence. However, it is at least arguable that violence on television has played a part in this dramatic rise.

Where is the violence on television? In 1995, researchers tabulated violence on television during a typical eighteen-hour broadcast period in Washington, D.C.[12] They looked at network television, cable television, and public broadcasting stations. Their analysis showed that the majority of violent acts occurred on cable television stations, in movies, and in cartoon shows. The most violent cartoons included *VR Troopers, X-Men,* and *GI Joe.* The most violent periods of day were six to nine A.M. and two to five P.M., the times when most children watch television.

Perhaps no aspect of television has received more intensive study than the relationship of violence on television to aggressive behavior in children. Hundreds of studies have made a compelling case that media violence greatly affects children. One has only to talk to preschool teachers for on-the-ground evidence of the extent to which children imitate television violence in their play. The specifics of the imitation parallel current popular programming. A few years ago, preschoolers were karate-chopping and fighting in the manner of the Teenage Mutant Ninja Turtles. Currently, they kick and fight in imitation of Power Rangers or the wrestlers of the World Wrestling Federation.

This tendency for children to learn behavior through imitation has been well studied. Researchers have shown video clips of aggressive behavior and then asked children to imitate the behavior.[13] Children's recall of the specifics of the behavior is impressive. Evidence also suggests that children recall with greater accuracy if they see that the aggressive behavior is rewarded.

A second study that added to the knowledge of children and television violence is a longitudinal study done in Canada in the 1970s, in which researchers had the unique opportunity to conduct a prospective study of children before they were exposed to television.[14] They compared a town that had no access to television with a nearby town that had television. Data was gathered on forty-five first- and second-grade children, using teacher and parent reports about their play. Television was then introduced to the first town. Data on children's play was again collected two years after the introduction of television. The first measurements showed significantly less aggressive play among the children who did not have access to television. The follow-up data indicated no difference in the aggressive play between the two groups. After two years of exposure to television, the children who previously had no access to television engaged in as much aggressive play as the control group. This study gives persuasive evidence about how television changes children's play.

Exposure to television violence also increases the viewer's apathy about or desensitization to aggression. Children who see violence on television may be less empathic toward real-life violence. They see violence as a norm and are less likely to intervene to stop aggression. This desensitization has been demonstrated in experimental situations.[15]

Finally, for children who have been exposed to real-life violence, television violence may represent a terrifying and realistic reenactment of their trauma. For these children, television violence precipitates acute anxiety and fear. It seems that exposure to real-life violence increases vulnerability to the effects of television violence. Family and community violence and television violence thus may have a synergistic effect on children.

It is important to note that the above research and descriptions pertain only to violence on television. There is perhaps an even greater risk to children of viewing violent or frightening movies on the VCR or in video games. Many children may be exposed to horror films or slasher movies, either without their parent's knowledge or because their parents do not fully understand the impact of such movies on young children. Horror films are particularly concerning because of their extremely graphic depiction of violence. Many children have reacted with symptoms of extreme stress and anxiety after viewing these movies.

Within the past ten years, violent video games have proliferated and have become increasingly realistic and gory. In many of these games, the player simply pulls the trigger and a body falls, gushing blood all over the floor. Their real-life quality is touted to sell the games. Critics of this genre of video games assert that they desensitize children, teaching them to fire at a human figure, and that the repetition of this activity reinforces the desensitization response. In fact, the technology behind these games has been used in simulated weapons training in the military.[16] An editorial in the *New York Times* pointed out that the fourteen-year-old boy (known to be a video game expert) who killed three people in the school shooting in Paducah, Kentucky, fired eight shots and hit eight people. The editorial noted, "He simply fired one shot at everything that popped up on his screen."[17]

Research on the effects of video game violence on children is in its infancy. Despite assertions about the links of violent video games and aggressive behavior in children, the supporting data is mixed.[18] Researchers generally agree that there are short-term effects: Children who play violent video games are more aggressive and desensitized to violence in the environment for a period of time after playing these games. The longer-term effects are unclear. Researchers also concur that these games have more pronounced and undesirable effects on younger children.

It is generally agreed that young children are the most vulnerable to the effects of all violent media programming: television, movies, and video games. They have neither the cognitive nor the emotional structures to understand the context of the violence. They do not understand the motives for the violence or grasp the consequences of the behavior. They are more likely to imitate the violence. Young children also have less ability to distinguish reality from fantasy. This is particularly evident in the way young children respond to scary programs. They don't understand that the story is "pretend" partially because it appears so real on television.

How is violence portrayed on the screen? Media violence is often disconnected from real consequences. It is "clean." There is a lack of blood, minimal suffering, and often, in the case of television and video games, the cartoon characters are invincible. The use of violence is frequently rewarded. There is a clear delineation between the "good guy" and the "bad guy," unlike in real life where there are often indistinct boundaries between good and bad. The good guy gets recognition, material reward, and increased status. The bad guy suffers and is made to look weak or stupid. The heroes may have good values and the message may be prosocial, but it is conveyed in ways that make violence seem justified. The violence may be humorous, as in the movie *Home Alone.* The message is that if violence is funny, it is acceptable.

Finally, children who see violence in the media begin to see the world as a dangerous place. Nowhere is this distorted view of the world more evident than in local newscasts. If a child were to form his or her opinions about the world solely from television newscasts, that child would believe that murders, rapes, and robberies occur everywhere and that it is only a matter of time before he or she falls victim to some act of aggression. This worldview is a troubling message to give young children and may discourage the kind of curiosity and exploration that lead to knowledge, self-confidence, and mastery.

Exposure to Real Violence

For too many children in this country, the violence they see is not confined to the television screen. Children may be direct victims of or helpless bystanders to violent incidents. In our training, we distinguish between community violence and domestic violence.

We define *community violence* as those incidents that occur on the streets, in neighborhoods, or in schools. Until the last few years, this type of violence was generally associated with neighborhoods containing high concentrations of families with few economic, emotional, or personal resources. Studies of children exposed to community violence usually focused on urban areas, such as the studies in Los Angeles, Boston, and New Orleans mentioned earlier. However, with the rash of school shootings in Columbine, Colorado; Paducah, Kentucky; Jonesboro, Arkansas; and in too many other places across America, the notion of what constitutes a safe community has changed. Neither social class nor geography insulates communities from violence. School shootings have occurred in affluent, predominantly white suburbs and rural areas.

We define *domestic violence* as abuse or threats of abuse between adult partners in the home. For many, the definition of domestic violence includes child abuse, sibling abuse, and elder abuse; in other words, any violence or abuse among family members. However, at the Child Witness to Violence Project, we describe domestic violence as the violence that occurs between adults or parenting figures. Twenty percent of adult women have experienced abuse at least once by a male partner. Estimates of the numbers of children who witness domestic abuse vary from three to ten million per year.[19] The reasons for this wide variation have to do with the precise definitions of domestic violence, the sampling techniques used by the interviewers, and the age of child inquired about. Nearly half the men who abuse their female partners also abuse their children.[20] Domestic violence is an "equal opportunity phenomenon," occurring in rural and urban areas, with less regard for class or ethnicity.

In truth, there are often fluid boundaries between the categories of children who are bystanders of violence and those who are victims of violence. In our project we have learned that many children who witness violence are also direct victims. This is particularly true when one considers child abuse. Children who live with domestic violence may grow up in households where there is violence throughout the household: Parents hit children; siblings hit one another. The lines between witnessing and being a victim are blurred.

MYTHS ABOUT CHILDREN'S EXPOSURE TO VIOLENCE

Two myths about violence in the lives of children and families bear careful consideration. The first myth is that violence is solely an urban problem. This myth is being revisited in the wake of the recent, high-profile school shootings, none of which occurred in an urban setting. Violence has touched the lives of families and children across this country, in rural areas, in the suburbs, in the inner city. Domestic violence can occur anywhere. Child abuse and community violence occur with more frequency in areas with high concentrations of people with inadequate housing and income and with high rates of drug use. This correlation speaks to the need for addressing the issues of poverty and inequity in this country as one strategy for reducing violence.

A second myth is that violence is a racial problem, existing primarily in minority communities. When people at the same income level are compared, there are few differences among races. This finding suggests that violence is a function of poverty, not race.

In 1986, a book titled *A Day in the Life of America* was published.[21] It was a coffee-table book, large, handsomely bound, and beautifully printed. It chronicled a twenty-four-hour period across the United States. As the book jacket explained, two hundred of the world's leading photojournalists were sent out all across the country on May 2, 1986, to take pictures from dawn through night. The book was a compilation of these pictures: photographs of family life and work; of people eating, socializing, and enjoying the outdoors. There was no text, only strong visual images of life in this country.

However, as this chapter has pointed out, this sanitized image of America is at odds with the reality. In truth, there is no such thing as a day in the life of America without violence. If the photographers had been accurate, they would have included photographs of street fights, shootings, domestic assaults, and child abuse. In summary, children live in a sea of violence and violent images. In the next chapters we will consider the consequences for children of growing up with violence.

CHAPTER 2

The Effects of Exposure to Violence on Young Children

In its coverage of the 1995 bombing in Oklahoma City, *Newsweek* magazine offered parents the following advice about their preschool-age children: "Turn off the TV and don't discuss the bombing. . . . Small children are usually oblivious to death, but they can be upset when they realize that adults, especially parents, are distressed."[1]

I read this advice ten days after the bombing as my colleagues and I were on our way to Oklahoma City to meet with early childhood providers and parents to assist them in helping young children cope with the aftermath of the bombing. In preparation we had talked to many parents, child care providers, and teachers who spoke of their children's awareness of the bombing. Children in one day care center used blocks to construct buildings and knock them down, commenting that the bombs had come. In another community, children voiced fear that their center might be bombed because they knew that children had been killed in a day care center in Oklahoma City. A parent reported that she was stunned to find her five-year-old daughter drawing a picture of bombs blowing up a building. Another parent described standing in the line at the grocery store checkout area with her four-year-old. On the news rack in front of them was *Newsweek* with the now famous photograph of the dazed and bloody fireman holding a baby. The child was fascinated with the picture and kept staring at it. As the parent attempted an explanation, the child said that he had heard about the bombing at his school. The parent had not been aware of the child's knowledge of this disaster. Clearly, as any parent or child care provider could attest, *Newsweek* had it wrong.

In our work with children at the Child Witness to Violence Project, we have learned two basic lessons about how early exposure to violence affects young children. The first and most troubling lesson is that it changes the emotional landscape for children by distorting their emerging view of the world and their place in it. For some children, this change becomes a fixed worldview. It lays the foundation for later behavioral and emotional problems. For others, the change may be more transitory and mediated by the response of adults. There is some evidence in new cognitive development research that this change may be physiological as well as emotional. The second lesson is that young children's understanding of events is shaped by their cognitive development. In the absence of careful adult explanations (and sometimes even with the most careful of explanations), children create their own meanings for events. These meanings may seem odd or irrational to adults, but for children they become an operating script for how the world works.

HOW EXPOSURE TO VIOLENCE CHANGES THE WORLD FOR CHILDREN

One day several years ago I received a telephone call from a woman named Carol, who was interested in volunteering in the Child Witness to Violence Project. She had read about us in the newspaper and thought our program sounded interesting. I asked about her interests and experience, and was surprised to hear that she was a graduate of an Ivy League business school, owned a consulting firm in the Boston area, and lived in an affluent suburb. We get a number of offers for volunteer assistance, usually from young people who want to be mentors or counselors and have some type of human service background. This offer was unusual.

We arranged a time for an interview. Carol was an attractive and well-dressed woman. I learned in talking with her that she had two children and that she was very busy with her firm, which was, by her report, quite successful. I began to talk with her about assisting us in fund-raising, since it seemed likely that we could make use of her entrepreneurial and marketing skills. Carol listened halfheartedly and finally said, "You know, I wish there had been something like this when I was a child, because something happened to me that I have never talked about with anyone before. In fact, I never thought about it much until I read about your program." With that, she began to tell me about the real reason she had come to talk.

Carol had grown up in a comfortable suburb of Cleveland, Ohio. She described her neighborhood as safe and orderly. She didn't remember any crime or other reason to be fearful before the day she came home from school and found her mother severely beaten and tied up in their home. As she began to describe this incident, it was as though she were seeing it again. She remembered that she had first gone into the house and found furniture and household possessions strewn all over the house. She described it as looking like a tornado had gone through the house. She frantically searched for her mother, and hearing sounds upstairs, found her bound to the center support beam in her bedroom. Her mother had blood on her face; an eye was badly swollen. Her clothes were torn. She freed her mother, who called the police. As she learned later, two men had broken into their home, raped and terrorized her mother, and tied her up before fleeing.

Carol was eight years old at the time of this assault. As she described it to me, it was as though it had happened last week. Her eyes were wide; her expression sickened as she described the way her mother's face looked. She said, simply, "My life was never the same again. My mother healed; we replaced everything that was broken; things were back to normal, except for me. It was just never the same. They were dealing with it the best they could," she said. "They probably thought it would be best for my sister and me if we just forgot about it. So no one talked about it again. In fact, I had almost forgotten about it until I read about your program." I asked her more about her memories and how she had thought of this horrible episode at the time. She replied that she had felt guilty, that if she had not been at school she might have been able to run for help. She described how she didn't want to go back to school for some time afterward. She was too scared that the assailants would return. She concluded by saying, "It's funny how one thing like that can change your life. I have never had anything scary happen to me since. I think I am happy, well adjusted, and successful. Yet I am not the same person I was before my mom was raped." She added, "This is the first time I have ever really told anyone what that experience was like for me. I wonder if it would have been different if I had seen a counselor at the time." With that, the meeting ended. I thanked her for her interest in the program, and she promised to contact me about a time to meet with my staff to talk about fund-raising ideas. We never heard from her again. I had wondered at the time about the real motivation for her interest in our program. Now I knew. She needed to be able to tell her story, and she needed a listener who could bear to hear it with her. Carol gives us an adult's perspective of how an overwhelmingly frightening event permanently changes the landscape for a person.

Lenore Terr, one of the most widely known researchers in the area of children and trauma, also writes about this phenomenon. She did her pioneering work in the early 1980s with a group of children who had been kidnapped.[2] The specifics of the kidnapping were memorable (and later made into a TV movie): Three men commandeered a busload of twenty-six children as the bus was on its way to a summer camp program in Chowchilla, California, a small farm town in the San Joaquin Valley. The kidnappers drove the bus and its occupants to a remote area and buried it for thirty-six hours in a huge pit. The adults and children were able dig their way to safety. There were no physical injuries, but the children were psychologically devastated by this experience. The town asked Dr. Terr to provide crisis psychiatric intervention to the children and their families.

Dr. Terr wisely recognized that this was also a unique opportunity to learn more about how children react to extremely terrifying events in their environments. These were children who had not had previous experience with danger or violence. Dr. Terr wanted to learn more about how unforeseen, random events such as this kidnapping affected children. She was also curious to see if age affected children's reactions to terror. In this group, the children on the bus ranged from age five to age fourteen, thus allowing her the chance to observe and interview a broad range of children. She interviewed them three times over the course of four years to document how their reactions changed over time.

When Dr. Terr began this research, the child psychiatry research community disagreed about the extent to which children were affected by being bystanders to overwhelmingly scary events. In general, it was believed that children's reactions to external events were more transitory than those of adults, that their age protected them from being permanently affected. Much of the psychiatric literature focused on the internal life of the child and the role of internal psychic conflicts, as opposed to the effects of external trauma on children.

However, considerable research was emerging from work with traumatized adults, specifically veterans of the Vietnam War, that documented how adults reacted psychologically in situations of chronic danger. There was ample evidence of the more permanent ways that adults could be affected: They suffered acute flashbacks and hallucinations, many had difficulty readjusting to life after the war, and some used alcohol and drugs to cope with the aftereffects. Researchers were also learning about the physiological side effects of constant exposure to danger: increased heart rates, chronic sleep difficulty, and changes in blood chemistry. This constellation of symptoms was named post-traumatic stress disorder (PTSD) and was included for the first time in the *Diagnostic and Statistical Manual of Mental Disorders* in 1980.[3] However, at that time, children could not be diagnosed with PTSD.

It was this question that Dr. Terr was interested in exploring: Can children suffer from PTSD? If so, how is it different from the adult version? Her answers to that question are thorough and compelling. In general she found that the children she studied were deeply scarred, psychologically, by this kidnapping. She elaborated on symptoms that she found in the children. These included repetitive traumatic dreams, cognitive confusion about the kidnapping or about events immediately preceding the kidnapping, post-traumatic play, which she described as being "repeated monotonously with no relief of anxiety," and reenactment of the event—for example, a child hiding every time she saw a school bus. Children described to her their intrusive and spontaneous memories of the kidnapping that interfered with their concentration in school. Furthermore, she found vestiges of these symptoms four years later when she reinterviewed the children.

In short, Dr. Terr found that children's responses to trauma were strikingly similar to adults' responses. The only differences between the Chowchilla children's responses and adults' responses to traumatic events seemed to be that children had less ability to sequence events in time or to accurately establish a time frame for the events, and that children did not describe unanticipated flashbacks in the same way adults did. While adults tend to "play back" traumatic events in sequence, children's memories seemed to be more fragmentary thoughts about the kidnapping. Dr. Terr's contribution to our understanding of the impact of traumatic experiences in children's lives is significant. Since then, many studies have added to our understanding of how trauma affects children. They have focused on natural disasters, such as floods, earthquakes, and hurricanes; war-related trauma; exposure to community violence; and exposure to interpersonal violence, such as domestic violence and child abuse. All have reinforced the point that children, even very young children, are profoundly affected by events in their environment.

One of Dr. Terr's most intriguing and sobering findings was about the ways in which the kidnapping experience altered the children's views of their own safety. She found that many of them suffered from nagging worry that it would happen again, and that for some children, their view of the future began to change. They could not imagine themselves ever feeling safe. A few children even had trouble imagining the future at all. Dr. Terr described this as "pervasive pessimism" or "a sense of foreshortened future," and she found this change in worldview to be the most enduring legacy of the kidnapping experience for children.

What does it mean for children to live with a sense of foreshortened future? Children seen in the Child Witness to Violence Project describe it in different ways. One family came to us after their nine-year-old daughter had been caught in the middle of gunfire that erupted between two rival gangs. Fortunately, she was minimally hurt, sustaining only superficial injuries to her foot. Her older brother and younger sister had been with her at the time of the shooting. We interviewed each of the children about their perspectives on this shooting. We were struck by the differences in how they thought about what had happened and how they coped with their fears. The direct victim of the shooting talked about her fears that it might happen again. She had been referred to a counselor at her school and in general seemed to be coping with the aftermath of the shooting. The youngest child admitted that she was scared at night, but then gave an elaborate explanation of how she arranged her many stuffed animals to protect her as she slept. For her, this ritual seemed to help. Her older brother Carlos was not as resourceful. In a videotaped interview, this ten-year-old boy described not being able to concentrate in school because he imagined the images of the young men who had shot his sister. Carlos said that he didn't go outside because he was scared. When asked by the therapist if he thought that he would be able to play outside next year, he replied, "No." She then asked him, "Do you think you'll be able to play outside again sometime?" He paused for a moment, dropped his voice, and said, "No." What is most striking on the videotape is his nonverbal language. As he is pondering this question about his future, he sinks in his seat and wraps his arms around himself. He seems to shrink before the viewer's eyes.

When we reviewed this videotape, we speculated about Carlos's future if he continued to feel so vulnerable and alone. As an emerging adolescent, one of his most important psychological tasks is to establish himself in the world of his peers and to form a sense of identity as a young man. One would hope that the efforts to establish this identity might include sports or hobbies or a part-time job, or perhaps a girlfriend. But what happens to him if he cannot comfortably be in the world? We thought about the power of gangs for a boy such as this. Gangs would offer the protection and the illusion of invincibility that this boy might crave. We could also imagine that Carlos might seek alcohol or drugs as an attempt to bolster his courage and eliminate his fears. We worried that he might decide to carry a weapon. What better way to shore up his fears than to arm himself against this scary world?

TRAUMA AND EARLY BRAIN DEVELOPMENT

In the last ten years there has been a dramatic growth in research on brain development and the role of early experiences. This research emphasizes the importance of the first three years and the critical window of opportunity that parents and child care providers have to ensure that their children will be successful in learning. The popularized use of this research has spawned a cottage industry of products designed to enhance the cognitive capacities of young children. Along with this trend has come research on the role of trauma or negative experiences on very young children. This research has revolutionized the way we think about infancy and early childhood. Through the advances of technology we now know that the infant's brain is taking in information and adapting to input from the moment of conception. Experiences in early life are far more important to the developing brain than was previously thought. And it has been clearly demonstrated that brutality, cruelty, and abuse leave indelible marks on the chemistry of a young child's brain.

Bruce Perry and colleagues at Baylor University have conducted numerous studies on the impact of abuse and trauma on the neurochemistry of the brain.[4] Their studies, although conducted largely with primates, demonstrate that frequent exposure to violence actually changes the structure of the developing brain.

These changes may result in neurochemical changes that increase impulsive and violent behavior. His conclusion is that chronic exposure to terrifying events leads to chronic overactivation of the human stress response, which in turn results in a permanent state of hyperarousal in the child. There is a subsequent increase in aggressive and impulsive behavior. In his words, "the terrorized infant becomes the terrorizing adolescent."

The implications of the correlation between early exposure to violence and permanent changes in brain chemistry are unclear, partially because of questions about generalizability of the findings (because many of the studies were done with animals) and partially because it is not clear whether these changes are permanent. It is certainly safe to say that growing up in a violent environment is not good for children, and that even infants may be adversely affected by early exposure to violence. And there is growing evidence that violence in the environment alters the neurochemistry in the brain. However, we must remember that most children who are exposed to violence early in their lives do *not* grow up to be violent or antisocial. They do not abuse their children or their partners. Thus, the pathways from exposure to violence and becoming a violent person remain unclear. We are not sure whether the changes in brain chemistry are irrevocable or what helps many children overcome the risks of early exposure.

Other researchers have addressed the question of whether infants and toddlers can be diagnosed with PTSD. Building on Lenore Terr's work with young children, Charles Zeanah and Michael Scheeringa have studied this youngest age group by conducting careful assessments, including videotaped observations of children with documented histories of abuse or victimization.[5] Focusing on children under four years of age, they found that these children showed symptoms of hyperarousal and avoidance of reminders of the trauma. They documented that young children who were exposed to traumatic events were likely to develop new fears and/or increased aggression after exposure. Finally, they found that it was not unusual for children exposed to trauma to lose a newly acquired developmental skill. For example, a child who had recently learned toilet skills would begin to wet the bed after exposure to a frightening event. The results of this study provided sufficient evidence for the inclusion of the diagnosis of post-traumatic stress disorder of infancy in the mental health diagnostic manual for infancy and early childhood.[6]

THE POWER OF MEMORY IN YOUNG CHILDREN'S LIVES

When we talk about the children we see in the Child Witness to Violence Project, we are frequently asked about their capacities to remember frightening events. Sometimes, the question about memory is couched in a parent's worries that talking about the terrifying event might bring back memories or make them more permanent. Sometimes, parents wonder if a child will remember an event later in life. Usually they hope that time will erase the memory. Occasionally, we hear questions about the accuracy of memory, particularly if the child is involved with legal testimony.

Researchers who have studied memory in young children tell us that children do not have full verbal memories of events before the age of two-and-a-half to three years. This capacity for verbal memories parallels the developing capacity for language. At these ages, children tend to remember extraordinary events rather than ordinary happenings. (One study found that the age at which children could recall birth of a sibling, a significant event in most families, was generally age four.)[7] For very young children, short-term recall is more reliable than longer-term memory. In addition, they may have difficulty remembering events in the proper time sequence. Young children are often better able to provide narrative memories if given a specific verbal cue. A treasured family story perfectly reflects these difficulties. One summer, our family took an extended vacation to visit relatives. For a two-week period, we spent one or two nights in a series of six different locations. Our younger daughter, who was five at the time, enjoyed chronicling the different places we visited, with particular emphasis on the food she had eaten at the various homes we had stayed in. She delivered the oral travelogue with great certainty and detail to anyone who asked. The only problem was that the order of the visits was completely out of sequence, as well as the specifics of what food she had eaten at which house. At times she could not even remember correctly where she had eaten breakfast the previous day. If we gave her certain cues, such as "What did you eat with your cousins David and Alexander?" her recall became more accurate. Her travel diary was the subject of much amusement for us, as she completely reinvented our vacation. However, its factual accuracy was seriously flawed.

Lenore Terr has found that traumatic memories are unlike the normal memories of childhood and are processed by young children in a different way.[8] She differentiates traumatic events in this way: "[A traumatic event] goes well beyond what was to be expected in the course of ordinary childhood and is horrifying and carries a threat against life, physical well-being or personal security."[9] In an interesting study on children's recall of the space shuttle *Challenger* disaster, she describes that the more emotionally involved the child was with the subject of the traumatic event, the more likely the child was to have "clear, brilliantly lit memories."[10] In this study, she compared children in New Hampshire who knew there was a New Hampshire teacher on board and saw the explosion on television, with a second group of children on the West Coast. These children first heard about the disaster verbally, without seeing images on television, and had no specific attachment to crew members. The New Hampshire children who saw the event on television had significantly clearer memories both during interviews at five to seven weeks after the explosion and at one year after.

Terr makes the important distinction between clear memories and accurate memories. Ten percent of the children reported some fact or sequence of the event inaccurately. Some children created unusual or idiosyncratic explanations for the explosion ("There was a large ice patch on the shuttle that caused it to malfunction"; "God did not want the shuttle to be in heaven"). However, emotional involvement was also related to accurate recall: The more emotionally involved the children were, the less likely they were to confuse the facts.

Another researcher, Max Sugar, described his work with five children under the age of five and their abilities to report traumatic memories.[11] One of the cases involved a twenty-six-month-old girl who gave a spontaneous and clear description of an airplane accident she had been in at age sixteen months. This researcher concluded that a child's ability to retain traumatic memories depends on the child's age at the time of the trauma, the attainment of language ability before the event, and the child's cognitive capability.

A child's ability to retain accurate long-term memories of events is more difficult to ascertain. What can we predict that a toddler who has witnessed a terrifying event will remember in ten years? The answer to this question probably depends on many variables: the extent of emotional involvement of the child, the level of language development, the security of the child's attachment to caregivers, and the chronicity of violent events in the child's life.[12] Researchers have studied the question of accuracy of children's longer-term memories and of suggestibility and children's memories.[13] Is it possible for others to influence what children remember? The findings are mixed. There seems to be evidence that adults can influence young children's memories of events by making suggestions or retelling the story for children. However, since these experiments are often conducted in laboratory or artificial settings, their relevance to situations of real trauma is questionable. These findings have added to the controversy about children's memories of sexual abuse and the possibilities that therapists or interviewers inadvertently shape children's responses.

In our work with young children, we have been amazed by the specificity and clarity of their memories about what they have seen or heard. They describe details; they talk about what they have heard; sometimes their descriptions include the use of other senses, such as touch or smell. One little girl who had seen her father beat her mother recalled that it happened during a thunderstorm. She commented that it "smelled like rain." Her mother told us that for several months afterward, her daughter would show excessive anxiety before a storm, saying that she did not like the smell. Young children's abilities to verbally communicate what they have seen may be limited. They are restricted both by immature expressive language and by the inability to fully understand what they have witnessed. We believe that children tell us about the aspects of events that are most upsetting or frightening to them and that this is influenced by their developmental stages. In our evaluation of the two-and-a-half-year-old, mentioned in the introduction, who witnessed the murder of his mother and reportedly called 911, the child said repeatedly, "My mommy was on the floor; my mommy was on the floor. She can't get up." We believe that this little boy perceived his mother's inability to get up as a willful abandonment, thus reflecting the salient developmental fears of two-year-olds who are negotiating the beginnings of separation and individuation from their primary caretakers. This child was less able to communicate what else had happened in the room or why his mother was on the floor. For him, this feature of the trauma was the most important.

HOW CHILDREN MAKE SENSE OF VIOLENT EXPERIENCES

As we are learning, children's abilities to understand or interpret a violent event depend on their ages and levels of cognitive development. Perhaps the best-known theory of children's cognitive development has come from the work of Jean Piaget.[14] Piaget describes a child's intellectual development as a sequence of stages that a child passes through on the way to achieving adult capacity for reasoning, abstract thinking, and understanding of cause and effect.

Piaget named the first stage of development the sensory-motor stage (from birth to age two), which involves the child's earliest perceptions of objects and people. Toward the end of this phase, children acquire object permanence, the capacity to remember an object or a person when it is no longer in sight. By the end of this stage, a child knows that his or her mother exists, even when she is not in the room, and that she will reappear.

Piaget describes the next stage of development as the preoperational stage, occurring between the ages of two and seven. In this stage, children begin to use language and to learn that objects have names. They develop a basic awareness of cause and effect; however, it is quite rudimentary. For example, when asked to explain why it gets dark at night, a four-year-old might reply, "Because my mom pulls the shade down." Simultaneous occurrences must be causally related. A child at this age can count from one to ten, or one to one hundred, but lacks the conceptual knowledge of what one or ten or one hundred is. A child's world at this stage completely revolves around him- or herself. A child can see the world only from a self-centered perspective and expects that others do as well. This egocentrism is the most striking aspect of this age and generally serves as an organizing or explanatory principle for many events. However, it also accounts for misunderstanding and misattribution of events. Children assume that they are to blame if things go wrong. They worry that their angry thoughts may hurt others.

Piaget describes the next stage as that of concrete operations, when a child is able to perform mental operations. At this stage, children can grasp the mathematical operations of addition, subtraction, multiplication, and division. This sets the stage for the development of formal operations (ages eleven to sixteen) and abstract thinking.

Piagetian concepts of children's cognitive development help us understand how young children make sense of violence in their lives. Without this framework, children's explanations may seem bizarre or irrational. In fact, adults frequently make the assumption that children think like adults do and therefore discount or ignore how children see the world.

In our work, we have learned that children's reactions to violent events are shaped by both cognition and emotion. Edward, age six, was referred to our project because he was both a victim of and a witness to a random shooting that occurred in the park across the street from his house, where he played regularly. One afternoon, gunfire erupted in the park. A young woman was killed and Edward was struck in the leg by a bullet. His response to this event seemed bizarre until we interviewed him more carefully about it. By his report, he went home and didn't tell anyone about his injury. He described taking off his bloody jeans, hiding them in the closet, and shutting himself up in the bathroom to clean off the wound in his leg, which fortunately was superficial. His mother discovered the injury because he didn't clean up the bathroom thoroughly. She found traces of blood on the floor and in the sink and soon discovered what had happened. When she brought Edward to see us, she was distraught at the fact that he hadn't told her about what happened. We were all perplexed by his silence. At first, he refused to talk about it. Then, as he developed a relationship with his counselor, Edward confided in her that the man who lived next door to him had just been to the hospital and had his leg amputated. His fear became clear: If he went to the hospital, he might also lose his leg. Edward did not have the reasoning skills to understand that his situation was entirely different from his neighbor's (who was diabetic). He simply assumed that if something was wrong with your leg and you went to the hospital, you would come home with no leg.

A second way we learned about the power of children's understanding of scary events was from Charlotte, a three-year-old girl whose mother, a university professor, came to see us because she had been the victim of domestic violence that Charlotte witnessed. The violence was severe, and Charlotte's mother went to court and had her husband arrested for assault. Her mother carefully explained to Charlotte that her father had hit her, had broken the law, and was going to jail. She explained that hitting was wrong and that he could not live in the house if he hurt others. She also expressed her hope that he would get help for this problem and might be able to come home again. She encouraged Charlotte to ask questions or to tell her if she was worried about her mom or her dad. Charlotte, a bright and precocious girl, considered this explanation carefully, remembering times she had seen her father hit her mother. She seemed relieved to talk about it. In her therapy session with me, she went over her mother's explanation again. She asked if I would write a letter to her dad in which she dictated the rules about not hitting and told him that he was bad because he hit her mom. She went on to say that she didn't like her dad. For many sessions, she repeated a ritual of either asking me to write a letter to her father (the letters were never sent or taken with her at the end of the session) or playing a game with the stuffed animals or puppets that involved their aggressive behavior. In this game, one of the animals was victimized by the other, by all manner of hitting and throwing the animal around. Sometimes she played the role of the victim and directed me in various ways to attack her stuffed animal. The dramatic moment of this sequence came when she announced loudly that the "bad puppet" would have to leave and would then be banished to the far corner of the office under a chair. This game was repeated on many occasions with minor variations, but always ended up with the puppet being banished. At first, I believed that this was a reenactment of the violence she had witnessed, a way for her to feel safe that her father was out of the house. But there was such a focus on the banishment of the puppet that I began to wonder if there was more meaning to it. Charlotte finally let me know about the real meaning of this play when she came in one week, obviously upset. She quickly told me that she was in trouble because she had hit her younger brother. It suddenly occurred to me that Charlotte might worry that she too might be banished from the house if she hit. I voiced that worry aloud and she froze. I then went on to say that children hitting and grownups hitting were very different. I explained that children were just beginning to learn rules and that they had a long time to practice them. Grown-ups knew the rules because they were grown up. I stated specifically that children would never have to leave their home if they hit their brothers or sisters because they were still learning about rules. Although Charlotte never responded directly to my statement, versions of it appeared in her next letter to her father. Soon she stopped playing the game with the animals. What I came to understand was that she, at age four, could not generalize about the rules or understand that rules were different for adults and children. She had one script for what happened when a person hits another.

Children's capacities to understand events depend on their abilities to take in and use information. These abilities change with age and development.

In our work with many children who have witnessed traumatic violence, we have come to believe that certain themes are almost universal in their responses. We hear variations on these themes in every child that we see. Sometimes children state meaning directly; at other times the themes emerge from their drawings or imaginary play.

The first theme we hear is that there is no safe place for these children. They begin to see their world as unpredictable, dangerous, and hostile. Carlos, who could not imagine going outside again, expressed this view of the world. For some children their homes are not safe because the violence comes from within. One little boy who lived with chronic domestic violence drew a picture of his house. It resembled a monster. The door looked like a mouth with teeth. The windows had eyes. He described that "hot oil" was spewing from the chimney. Another window had "thorns around it." This house was terrifying. He then drew his sister and himself running from the house. As if the image of the house wasn't clear enough, he drew himself with no hands and his sister without hands or feet. These were maimed children running from a house of horrors.

Other children demonstrate a constant watchfulness, as though they are on guard for the next bad or dangerous thing that might happen. They are acutely sensitive to sounds or unexpected noises. They scan the environment for trouble. Daquan, who had witnessed his mother's murder, constantly jumped when the man in the office next door sneezed. "What's that?" he asked, or, "Who is in there?" A direct answer would reassure him temporarily, but when he heard the noise again, he was compelled to check it out. If someone could come onto his street and shoot his mother, how could any place be safe?

This kind of hypervigilance takes a toll on children. It likely affects their nervous systems as they experience this chronic overactivation of the neurochemical stress response. It's as though they are permanently poised for fight or flight, a lifelong state of arousal, with the accompanying surges of adrenaline. It interferes with their abilities to accomplish learning tasks in school. These children are distractible and unfocused. They do not complete assignments. They may be highly active and restless. They notice every visitor who comes into the room; they get distracted by noise or by a change in schedule. Some children describe being preoccupied with thoughts or memories of the traumatic event. One seven-year-old girl told us that whenever things were quiet in school she would remember what happened to her mother (who had been assaulted by her father). One can imagine the ways in which this child worked to avoid quiet time in school: She was constantly disruptive and annoying to the other children.

Witnessing violence affects a child's developing capacity for reality testing, for understanding what is real and what is fantasy. This is a developmental issue particularly for preschoolers, who are only beginning to make the distinction between what is real and what is make-believe. Children of this age enjoy imaginary companions and worry about ghosts under the bed. They are not sure whether dreams are real or not. Their inner world may contain a variety of fears and worries. Children of this age wonder if their secret wishes have real power: "If I don't like my sister, will she die?" For this age group real-life violence may be overwhelmingly frightening, as it becomes confused with the child's inner fantasies and fears. In addition, explanations given to children of this age about why someone was injured or died are often confused with fear or fantasy. For example, a five-year-old child referred to our project had been told that God took her neighbor (who had been shot) to heaven. This child refused to go inside a church because she had also been told that God lived in the church and she was afraid she would be taken.

Another theme we hear from young children is that adults are not emotionally available, and cannot offer protection. For toddlers who are beginning to experiment with autonomy, an essential component of their successful explorations of the larger world is the security of a parent who supports and encourages this autonomy and serves as an anchor. When violence disrupts this connection, children may respond by withdrawing, avoiding exploration, and ceasing to see adults as protective. Children feel alone and vulnerable. They draw pictures of their families in which the parents are smaller than the children or they draw adults as superheroes, expressing the wish for all-powerful protection.

The logical corollary of this theme, of course, is that children come to believe that they must protect themselves and those that they love. This psychological shift was demonstrated to me in talking with a four-year-old and his mother. This boy had seen many arguments between his parents, some of which ended in physical fights. His mother had been seriously injured on several occasions. As she described one of these fights to me, I saw her son get up from his seat and move toward her. He put his hand on her knee and said, "Don't worry, Mom, I won't let it happen again." It was both poignant and scary. At age four, this child already felt the responsibility to protect his mother. I wondered if in looking at this boy, I was looking at a member of the next generation of abusers. We have learned that it is more comfortable for many children to choose aggression than to experience vulnerability. It is better to strike first rather than to wait passively.

Many children play out fantastic and elaborate sequences of fighting and aggression. The puppets in our offices help children express the aggression in the safety of a therapeutic space. The favorite puppets are a shark with a large mouth and exaggerated teeth; a dinosaur, also with sharp teeth; and a tiger. Children use the puppets to gobble at smaller puppets; they hurl them across the room; they beg the therapist to engage in hand-to-hand combat using the puppets. One of the psychological tasks for all young children is to learn to manage aggressive impulses in socially appropriate ways. Many of these urges are internally driven and are a normal part of a child's development. But when the inner aggression is fueled by instances of external aggression, a child is easily overwhelmed. One senses that these aggressive urges are literally bubbling over for these children. We then wonder about the connection of these early experiences with violence and adolescents' violent or antisocial behavior. The seeds of violence are sown early in life.

This thesis is explored in depth in a book titled *Ghosts from the Nursery: Tracing the Roots of Violence,* by Robin Karr-Morse and Meredith Wiley.[15] Using the new brain research as a central theme, these writers review a large number of studies focusing on infants and young children's experiences with violence, neglect, and prenatal exposure to drugs. They postulate that these experiences are the critical link to violent behavior in adolescence and adulthood. The authors then make a powerful case for increased support of young children and parents by defining this early intervention support as a form of crime prevention.

In summary, children's exposure to violence exacts emotional, social, cognitive, and physiological costs. There is no age at which a child seems to be immune from this exposure. The notion that age somehow protects a child from the effects of violence in the environment does not hold up under scrutiny. However, we also know that children are affected in a range of ways and that not all children are doomed to a future of violent behavior or emotional turmoil. The challenge lies in better understanding how children might be protected from the adverse effects of violence.

CHAPTER 3

When Home Isn't Safe

Children and Domestic Violence

When we speak to groups of parents or professionals about our work with children who witness violence, they frequently ask about our findings: What kinds of violence are children being exposed to? What is the worst form of violence for children? As we have accumulated experience with many children and families, we have reached conclusions about the answers to those questions. Despite the fact that the Child Witness to Violence Project began as a response to children's exposure to community violence, we have learned that children are most affected by exposure to the more private and insidious violence that occurs inside their homes. Domestic violence, violence that occurs between adult caregivers in the home, seems to be the most toxic form of exposure to violence for children. Furthermore, we now believe that young children are far more likely to be exposed to violence in the home than to violence on the street. For many children, the first lessons they learn about violence are not from television or from the streets, but from their parents. These lessons are generally the wrong lessons: that it is acceptable to use threats or force to get one's way, that violence has a place in an intimate relationship, that adults can hurt one another and not apologize or take responsibility for their actions.

This is not to say that exposure to murder or mayhem on the

streets does not affect children. Children talk extensively about their fear of going outside or going to school, their worries about their parents and families, and their sense of vulnerability. Parents speak with frustration and hopelessness about not being able to let their children go to the park or having to impose limits on their children, not because they do not trust them, but because they do not believe the environment is safe. Sometimes these limits become the source of conflict, as young children want to spend time with peers and parents are frightened to allow their children to pursue this age-appropriate desire.

The violence that occurs within the home, however, is worse for children. They are more intensely affected and the consequences last longer. This form of violence has been hidden from the public eye. There has been little media attention to domestic violence unless it was a fatal or particularly horrific episode of abuse. In retrospect, as we looked back upon our initial expectations of whom we would serve in the Child Witness to Violence Project, we realize that we, too, underestimated the prevalence of domestic violence. It was easier to look at the violence on the street than to face the horrors of what people who ostensibly love one another could do to each other within the seclusion of their homes.

The conspiracy of avoidance was particularly obvious in the case of Charles and Carole Stuart in 1989. This case, which drew national attention, involved the murder of a young pregnant woman. Her husband reported that they had been assaulted and robbed by armed black men as they drove home from childbirth classes at a local hospital. The murder occurred in a predominantly black neighborhood of Boston. The coverage of the case played on stereotypes: Black men are dangerous, especially to white women; black neighborhoods are notoriously unsafe for white people. Police began a massive hunt for the assailant and arbitrarily rounded up many young black men to interview. They made a quick arrest and were prepared to close the case when the husband committed suicide by jumping off a bridge. It was then revealed that Charles Stuart had murdered his wife as part of a scheme to collect insurance money. The aftermath of that highly publicized event was a soul-searching debate about the assumptions we make about people and behavior.

In a similar manner, we discovered that it was easier for the Child Witness to Violence Project to focus on the effects of community violence on children than to look at the violence within children's homes. We wanted to disbelieve or minimize the stories that children told. These cases of domestic violence raised complex and difficult issues. They almost always involved other systems: police, children's protective services, and the courts. Sometimes it was hard to tell the "good guys" from the "bad guys." We found ourselves angry with mothers for staying in the relationships, for not protecting their children. We felt helpless because there were no easy solutions for most of these cases. We were forced to look at our own attitudes and beliefs about relationships, conflict, and what is best for children.

Domestic violence (also termed spousal abuse, partner violence, family violence, intimate partner violence, and wife beating) technically refers to any act of interpersonal violence between or among family members, including child abuse. For the purpose of this book, domestic violence refers to threats of intimidation or violence or actual acts of violence between adult partners. In our project, the large majority of cases involve acts of violence or threats made by men against women. The national statistics of reported domestic violence incidents bear out this trend. According to the Bureau of Justice Statistics at the U.S. Department of Justice, 85 percent of the victims of domestic assault are women.[1] Domestic violence is sometimes described as a "women's issue" or a "feminist concern." From our experience, we believe that it is everyone's problem and a critical issue for children. For anyone who is concerned about youth violence or violence prevention, the issue of domestic violence must be among the first to receive attention.

Wife abuse is not a new phenomenon. The current attention paid to this issue, however, is a result of the resurgence of the feminist movement in the 1960s and 1970s. In her book, *Heroes of Their*

Own Lives: The Politics and History of Family Violence, Linda Gordon provides a fascinating historical perspective on the evolution of domestic violence as a social problem.[2] Her book provides an analysis of 1,500 child abuse and neglect records from Boston-area social service agencies between 1880 and 1960. During this time, there was no systematic protocol for inquiring about or documenting the presence of domestic violence. Even without systematic assessment, however, as many as one-third of the records surveyed mentioned abuse of women. Nevertheless, the primary focus was always on the direct abuse or neglect of the children. Case records elaborately documented children's cleanliness, injuries, illnesses, and malnutrition. Wife abuse was neither identified as a problem in its own right nor directly addressed by social service agencies. At varying times, caseworkers responded with moral judgment of mothers and fathers, with efforts to reform behavior, or with psychological condemnation, particularly of women for their failures as parents. The fact that they were also being abused was simply overlooked, even by the women themselves. In Gordon's findings, women came forward for help with their children, but rarely mentioned their own abuse.

Throughout much of the twentieth century, the courts routinely upheld sexually discriminatory laws reflecting what was understood to be the proper relationship between men and women, relationships that were based on English common law. This body of law held that women (and children) were the husband's property. These laws had far-reaching implications for women in terms of divorce law, domestic relations, and definitions of marital rape. The abuse of women was not acknowledged, much less labeled as criminal behavior. World War II set the stage for dramatic changes in relationships between women and men. As many men left to fight overseas, women took more responsibilities at home. With this shift and with postwar prosperity, women became less dependent on men, both financially and psychologically. The seeds of the women's movement were sown.

In the early sixties, with the beginning of the feminist movement, a new consciousness arose about violence within marital relationships. For the first time, this problem was framed as a social problem, as opposed to a psychological or interpersonal one. This important shift in definition laid the groundwork for the beginning of the battered women's movement in the 1970s. By this time, marital violence was defined as an abuse of power, to be viewed in the context of our tradition of patriarchal law.

This shift in the definition of marital violence from personal to social problem redrew the lines between private behavior and public interest. Victims of domestic violence were heard in many forums. Laws were created to protect their rights and to criminalize wife abuse. An array of services, shelters, and counseling programs were created to serve victims and perpetrators of domestic violence. In short, the notion of a man's house being his castle dramatically changed as his private behavior landed in the public domain.

The history of public awareness of children as the hidden victims of domestic violence is even shorter than the history of awareness of domestic violence. Before 1990 there is scant mention in the child mental health literature of child witnesses to domestic violence. Even within the battered women's movement, there was little mention of children and few programmatic resources for them. The early advocates for victims of domestic violence believed that the focus should be on women's safety. Diverting resources to children reinforced the patriarchal attitudes of women's needs being placed last. In addition, there was the pressure of limited resources. Shelters operated on limited budgets and there was understandable reluctance to divert money to children's programming.

Services for the children of battered women began to grow in the early 1990s. This growth was probably due to two influences. First, there was a growing awareness in the child mental health community of the devastating impact of environmental trauma on children.[3] Research yielded valuable findings about the impact of early experiences on brain development and child functioning. The second factor that supported the growth of children's services was the influx of federal and state money for services to battered women. Perhaps the largest amount of money was made available by the federal government through the passage of the Violence Against Women Act in 1994, which provided more than one billion dollars for increased funding to battered women's shelters, training for police and prosecutors, and legal resources for prosecuting domestic violence cases. This increase in resources has spilled over into children's services. Children of battered women are no longer the hidden victims.

DOMESTIC VIOLENCE: A LEGACY OF SECRET AND SHAME

Today, domestic violence is widely recognized and accepted as a pressing family problem. Extensive media campaigns, television dramas, novels, and magazine articles have made domestic violence an issue for our society. However, women continue to tell us that they are ashamed to admit that they are in abusive relationships, particularly if children are involved. Obstacles to seeking help include the fear of being judged a failure, fear of losing one's children, the sense of deserving the abuse, and the fear of being blamed for not leaving the relationship. In our interviews with women, they express deep shame; they listen carefully to our questions to find evidence of our judgment or condemnation. As they recount instances of abuse, they look to see if we are repulsed or disbelieving. Despite the increasing societal recognition of domestic violence, many women continue to find it unacceptable to disclose their personal struggles.

In a pattern that is consistent with this sense of self-blame and self-hate, some women make their way to our services precisely because children are involved. When we ask why a woman is seeking services now, she tells us that she is concerned about the children. In other words, some women cannot seek help for themselves, but they will go public about the violence on behalf of children. This is the same pattern Linda Gordon found in her research on the late 1800s.

Another important dimension of a woman's decision to seek help is the way in which her culture views marital relationships and efforts to seek help outside the family. Several women seen in the Child Witness to Violence Project have told us that their religion prohibits leaving their husbands or that their marriage vows dictate that they stay in the relationship at any cost. In some cultures, spousal separation is shameful and divorce is rare. The notion of counseling is unheard of. To talk about family problems outside the home brings disgrace on the family.

CHILDREN AND CONFLICT IN THE HOME

Conflict is an inherent part of family relationships. Most if not all parents have raised their voices toward their spouses or children. Couples argue, children fight, parents yell. How does this conflict affect children? At what point does parental arguing become abusive or harmful to children? This question has been carefully studied and the findings are interesting. According to Mark Cummings and his colleagues, who have published extensively in this area, children, even in their infancy, show reactions of distress when they are exposed to "background anger," defined as adults verbally arguing and yelling.[4] In one series of experiments, twenty-month-old toddlers showed increased amounts of aggression with their playmates after they had been exposed to anger or loud arguing between adults.[5] This research underscores the fact that even very young children are aware of conflict in the home and that the conflict affects their behavior.

Another interesting dimension of this research is children's response to conflict. Children are likely to become involved in marital conflict by attempting to distract, comfort, or solve problems for the arguing parents. These responses can be seen in children as young as age two. By age five or six, children actively attempt to mediate parent arguments.

One might assume that children who grow up in homes where there is constant arguing or yelling would adapt. They would get used to it, and therefore be less affected. Contrary to expectations, however, Cummings discovered that repeated exposure to parent arguing does not diminish children's reactions. Children react more strongly by becoming more anxious and aggressive. The notion of becoming desensitized to parental fighting was not supported by this research.

Finally, Cummings and colleagues have found that if parents resolved the arguments, children were much less likely to be affected.[6] Even partial resolution, such as changing the subject or agreeing to drop the argument, seemed to dramatically reduce the impact on children. In their simulated experiments with children, they instructed some of the adults to resolve arguments in front of children and others to leave the room and return with indications that the fight was over. Although children who had heard the resolution to the argument benefited the most, the stress of all children was markedly reduced.

The take-home message for all parents from this series of studies is that marital conflict is not inherently bad for children. Children may even learn positive and prosocial lessons from seeing their parents argue and then resolve the conflict. If the argument is resolved, children can cope. If the arguments are chronic and unresolved, however, children react negatively. In Cummings's research, fighting that included physical aggression was much more psychologically harmful for children than verbal arguing. This is not surprising, but the consistency of their findings builds a powerful case for the ways in which physical fights or even threats of personal injury overwhelm children's abilities to cope. Children who lived with physical aggression were more likely to blame themselves and to see themselves negatively. This distorted self-appraisal affected children in all areas of social functioning.

Since 1990, nearly 100 studies of the effects of exposure to domestic violence on children have been published, most focusing on children between the ages of six and seventeen.[7] These studies thoroughly analyzed the risks of domestic violence for children. It is quite clear that exposure to domestic violence affects children in a range of deleterious ways. It affects their emotional development, their social functioning, their ability to learn and focus in school, their moral development, and their ability to negotiate intimate relationships as adolescents and adults. It is associated with greater rates of juvenile delinquency, antisocial behavior, substance abuse, and mental illness. It also increases the risk of direct physical injury. Children who are bystanders to conflict often become the direct victims of abuse. Young children lack the ability to remove themselves from the fighting: A toddler clings desperately to his mother; an infant is held by her mother who is being beaten. Older children may try to intervene and are injured as a result of their attempts to mediate or protect.

Why is domestic violence so toxic for children? Researchers who have studied this question enumerate several characteristics. Exposure to a violent event is more psychologically threatening for children, especially young children, if the child perceives him- or herself to be in danger, if the child perceives that the caretaker is in danger, and if the child is physically close to the violent event.[8] All these attributes apply to situations involving domestic violence. In one study, researchers looked at records of children who had been diagnosed with PTSD.[9] Because these children were in the court system, the researchers had access to detailed and extensive records on the children, some of which extended over a number of years. They were curious to learn more about what stresses might be most strongly correlated with the child's diagnosis of PTSD. They found that two factors were the strongest predictors: a history of sexual abuse and witnessing chronic domestic violence. In fact, exposure to domestic violence seemed to be more harmful overall than being a direct victim of child abuse. This reminds us that if the violence is close at hand, if it involves caretakers, if it puts the child at harm, the child is much more likely to suffer serious and long-lasting emotional consequences.

Another powerful by-product of domestic violence between parents is the lesson children learn about the use of force and intimidation. Young children learn social roles by imitating what they see and hear. They dress up like Dad, do housework with Mom, practice the moves of cartoon figures on television. If children observe that physical force is a part of their parents' relationship, they will also imitate this behavior. In violent homes, children learn that aggression is a part of intimate relationships, or that it is acceptable to relieve stress by yelling or threatening another family member. It is normal to use force to get one's way, and no apologies are necessary. When these children enter day care or preschool and hear rules such as "Use your words, not your hands" or "No hitting allowed," they have no context to rely on. These rules make no sense. Instead, these children have constructed their own understanding of the social order: Might makes right. An accidental bump from another child is interpreted as purposeful aggression. One must always be on guard for violence. Thus, a child who grows up with violence behaves in a distrustful, aggressive fashion. This stance works at home, but fails miserably in preschool settings.

Perhaps the greatest distinguishing feature of domestic violence for young children is that it psychologically robs them of both parents. One parent is the terrifying aggressor; the other parent is the terrified victim. For young children,who depend exclusively on their parents to protect them, there is no refuge. These situations are different from those of families who face community violence. In most of those cases, parents are not fearful for their own lives and can be both heroic and resourceful in their efforts to protect their children. (This is not to imply that women who are victims of domestic violence are not heroic and resourceful; however, if they are fighting for their own survival, there are limits on what they can do to protect their children.) Parents' emotional availability makes a big difference in how children respond to the trauma of a violent event. In the Child Witness to Violence Project we learned about the buffering effects of parents in memorable ways.

One of the first cases referred to us was that of Lisa, a nine-year-old girl who lived with her family in a tough Boston neighborhood where street crime was common. Lisa woke one night to see a man at her window, attempting to open her screen. She was terrified by this vision and began to scream for her mother. By the time her mother entered the room, there was no sign of the intruder. The mother reassured Lisa that it must have been a bad dream. Lisa was not convinced, and spent the remainder of the night in a terrified state. The next morning, her mother checked the window and found signs of an attempted forced entry. Lisa's nightmare had been real.

Within a week of that incident, Lisa became afraid to go out of the house. She begged her mother to change bedrooms; she could not sleep at night. When she began to miss school, her mother took Lisa to her pediatrician. The mother was exasperated, saying that she needed help in convincing Lisa to forget about this incident. The mother had bought strong latches for all the windows and she thought the house was safe from intruders. She believed that the best thing to do was to stop thinking and talking about the incident. It was apparent, however, that no amount of security could help Lisa feel safe. The pediatrician asked for a consultation from our program and I agreed to sit in as the doctor talked with Lisa about her fears.

Before the meeting, the doctor and I agreed that he should be the person to interview Lisa since he had known her for many years. With her mother and me in the room, he gently asked her to talk about what had happened. Lisa talked about waking up to see this scary face at the window. She became animated as she remembered the man's face and the sounds of him cutting the screen. She reviewed her confusion and disbelief when he disappeared. Maybe it had been a dream, she speculated. However, with the corroborating evidence, she now felt terrified that he would return. She tried to imagine what he would have done if he had entered the room. She talked about seeing scary movies where girls are kidnapped and killed. Within a few days, she had begun to worry that he was following her, and she was afraid to go to school. She also talked about how hard it was to close her eyes at night. We understood that she was not sleeping, which further contributed to her reluctance to go to school. The doctor asked many questions about how often she thought about the man at the window, when she was most afraid, and what her greatest fears were. In short, he allowed her to talk openly about the incident from her perspective, and he validated her feelings. He neither minimized her feelings nor attempted to give reassurance. He just listened.

As the mother heard her daughter explain what this incident

had done to her, she became visibly upset. Speaking through her guilt, she explained that she had thought it would be best if they didn't dwell on what had happened, and therefore, she had not allowed her daughter to express how scared she was. As Lisa spoke directly about the aftermath of this incident, her mother also became angry. She revealed for the first time that she had a good idea of who the intruder was. By her report, their house bordered an area that was known for drug selling, and the suspected intruder was a drug dealer who was known in the neighborhood. In an animated and determined voice, she told her daughter that she would make sure that this did not happen again. Lisa's mother was a large woman who by her own description could be forceful if necessary. I began to worry that she might take matters into her own hands in ways that were potentially dangerous for her. She was resolute, however, that she would take care of matters. As she provided reassurances, I observed that Lisa, who had been tense and withdrawn, was now relaxed.

The doctor then asked Lisa what she thought might be helpful in a plan to get her back to school. He discussed a plan with Lisa and her mother to change her bedroom around so that her bed was facing away from the window. (This was Lisa's request.) He asked them to return in two weeks for a follow-up session. The family did not return, but phoned instead to say that Lisa was much better and had returned to school.

How did this encounter help Lisa? I observed Lisa's nonverbal behavior carefully during the interview and was struck by her connection to her mother. Although the doctor was asking the questions, Lisa talked to her mother about her feelings. She wanted her mother to know what this experience had been like for her. I was also impressed by the power of this mother's reassurances. It was evident that Lisa savored her mother's fury. Her mother's absolute confidence that she could take care of this situation was the optimal intervention for Lisa. Children want (and need) to believe that their parents can protect them. This mom was eloquent in that regard. I believe that her strength was contagious and helped Lisa conquer the fears she had developed.

This case shows how parents can psychologically help their

children cope with the aftermath of trauma. If the parents are themselves traumatized, however, their capacity to emotionally protect their children is often compromised. The double jeopardy of exposure to domestic violence is that children are both directly traumatized by their exposure to trauma and robbed of the refuge of their parents. Consider the following story.

Michelle, a twenty-eight-year-old mother of three children —Mark, age seven, Sally, age six, and Eric, age four—brought her children to the Child Witness to Violence Project for counseling services at the suggestion of the local battered women's shelter where she had been staying. The shelter staff was concerned about the children's behavior, and particularly about Mark, who was very aggressive and moody in the shelter. At the first evaluation session, we began by seeing the mother and children together. This standard practice gives children a chance to feel more comfortable in the setting and to discuss with all family members the reason for seeking services from us. We decided to assign two therapists to this family because of the number of children. My colleague asked the mother to tell us something about why she had brought the children in. The mother began by telling us that they had lived in a small town about forty miles from Boston until two weeks ago, when she fled from her husband and came to Boston. Michelle, who sat hunched in the chair, then told a horrific story about the abuse that led to her decision to leave home. She described that her husband had hit her for years, culminating in an incident in which he attempted to strangle her with an extension cord. This incident happened one morning after the older children had gone to school. Eric was at home and witnessed the event. Michelle recounted every detail of what led up to this assault and told us about how she had been able to break loose by kicking her husband. She grabbed Eric and fled from the house, hailing a taxi that took her to the older children's school. From the school she called the police. The police transported her and her children to the domestic violence shelter. She later learned that her husband had been arrested and charged with attempted murder.

As she told the story, I observed the children. They began the session by sitting quietly in three chairs. However, as Michelle began to talk, the children fidgeted and began to bicker with each other. Mark reached over and hit Sally. Eric moved to the play area and looked at the toys. Soon all three children were in the play area. The older children began to pull toys off the shelf. A dispute broke out over one toy. In a flash, they began to throw them at each other. Eric sat in the corner, looking stunned. This escalation in action and aggression took place within a five-minute span. The children became so disruptive that I could not hear Michelle talk. She made no attempt to intervene or calm her children. She finally stopped talking when Mark threatened to pull a bookcase over onto the floor.

As difficult as it was for me to sit passively, I knew that the children's behavior was communicating a powerful message and that I should refrain from intervening unless the situation was dangerous. This unfolding of events gave us rich information about the family. We later realized that the increasing chaos that the children produced was their way of telling their mother that they could not bear to hear the story she was telling. It was too overwhelming. They got her to stop by using the time-honored strategy of escalating their misbehavior to the point of danger. Obviously they had used this strategy before and it was a familiar sequence of interactions for them. It worked. Michelle stopped talking and began to yell at the children to clean up the mess they had made.

Equally striking to me was Michelle's single-minded focus on retelling her story to the extent that she seemed completely unaware of her children. As she told the story, she was reliving the horror and was unable to tune in to her children's distress. She was so traumatized that she could not see how scared and upset her children were to hear the story told again. We have learned from many of the women we work with that this numbness and decreased ability to recognize when children are frightened or distressed is a hallmark of their trauma. Despite her good intentions, Michelle's ability to emotionally protect her children was compromised by her own experiences with violence.

This case illustrates the particular risks of exposure to domestic violence for children and how parental response makes a difference. When parents are overwhelmed, they are unable to read their children's cues of distress, and the situation often deteriorates rapidly.

The following stories show how individuals in families struggle with the existence of violence within the home, particularly the relentless toll that this behavior takes on children. In addition, these stories provide a reminder that domestic violence cuts across all social classes.

THE STORIES OF JENNA AND BEN

We received a request from a family court judge to help determine what kind of visitation schedule should be established for two children who had witnessed physical violence between their parents. They were in the custody of their mother; their father was seeking access to his children by asking the court to set up a schedule for visits. The judge wanted to impose a schedule that was fair to the parents but that also took into account the children's emotional reactions to the violence. In order to make informed recommendations, we arranged to spend time with each child and each parent to get to know them, to hear from each member of the family about their perspectives on the parents' conflict and their ideas for how the visits should be scheduled.

The family lived in a wealthy suburb of Boston. Both parents worked full-time. The father was an attorney; the mother, a college professor. The children—Jenna, age nine, and Ben, age seven—attended private day school. The third child, six-month-old Jacob, was not part of the request for visitation. Both parents agreed that he was too young to be a part of the visitation plan for the immediate future. Before we met the family, we learned from the court that there had been at least one incident of physical violence between the parents that had resulted in police intervention. In fact, Ben had called 911 during the fight. A police report was sent to us, along with a copy of the judge's temporary custody order. The report documented injuries to the mother and the resulting arrest of the father. He was held for a few hours. His wife asked that he be released, on the condition that he not stay at home. Other than this meager information, we knew little about the family.

We interviewed the father and the mother separately, asking them each the same questions: Could they tell us about the marital conflict? What was it about? How long had it been going on? What did the children understand about the conflict? Who talked with the children about it? How did the children seem to be affected? We also asked each parent about his or her relationship with their children. We asked them to describe the children, to talk about what they liked to do with the children, about each child's strengths and talents, what concerns they had about the children, and what their ideas were about a good plan for visitation.

As is often the case with parents who are locked in struggle, their perspectives and recommendations were dramatically different. The father, whom I interviewed first, was bitter and angry about being denied access to his children. He saw this refusal as an attempt by the mother to gain power and turn his children against him. He admitted that the parental relationship had been stormy, with angry fights and poor communication. When asked about the physical violence, he was dismissive. He told me that things got out of hand once in a while, but that she was an equal participant. He explained that the incident involving the police had been overblown. They had had a fight, she had picked up a knife, and he had tried to protect himself, resulting in injuries to both of them. When asked specifically about other incidents of physical fighting, he said that there had been one or two times when they had pushed or grabbed each other. There had been no injuries and to the best of his knowledge, the children had not been aware of these fights because they usually happened in the evening after the children were in bed.

I then asked him about his children and how he saw their strengths. He described them both as smart, doing well in school, and enjoying sports. However, as I asked more specific questions, he said that he actually did not spend much time with them because of the demands of his job. His description of his children was vague and without animation. He wanted to change the subject to address his anger at being denied access to the children. I also asked in some detail about his work and his background. By his report, he was a hard-working and successful lawyer. When he was a child, his family had had little money; he was the first member of his family to graduate from college. He worked hard to get through law school. He was particularly proud that he had been able to afford to buy a new home in the past year in an expensive neighborhood. He mentioned also his satisfaction in being able to send his children to private school, an advantage he had not had.

I then interviewed the mother. As I expected, her story was quite different. She said that their relationship had begun to deteriorate when he was in law school. She taught part-time and provided most of the care for their young daughter Jenna. Her husband had little to do with Jenna and provided no support at home. She resented his lack of involvement. They argued about this from time to time. Occasionally the arguments were heated. She recalled the first time he pushed her. She was shocked and left home for a couple of days to stay with her mother. By the time Ben was born, she described her marriage as "miserable." She barely saw her husband; their only communication seemed to be through their fights. There were occasional episodes of fighting that escalated to physical abuse. She reported that he would berate her, and sometimes she would be so angry that she slapped him. On one occasion, he pushed her against the kitchen cabinets and bruised her arm badly. She remembered being worried that her colleagues would ask about the bruises, but she knew that she could easily make up a story. She also remembered being relieved that the bruises weren't on her face. It would have been more obvious and harder to lie if the injury had been on her face.

The mother described the incident involving the police. By her report, her husband had listened to a telephone message for her from a male colleague. He became suspicious, accusing her of having an affair. The fight, which began in the kitchen, quickly escalated. He grabbed her by the hair and took out a kitchen knife.

She was terrified and called to the children to summon the police. The baby was asleep upstairs; she did not know where the older children were at the time, but she remembered that she was afraid for her life. She managed to kick the knife out of his hand and run out the door. The police arrived as she was running from the porch. They saw evidence of the fight in the kitchen and made an arrest on the spot. The father was removed and put in jail.

Afterward, she collected the children, who were terrified. She made the decision at that point to leave her husband. She told me that the intensity of his anger was unlike anything she had experienced before, and she knew that she could stay with him no longer. Despite her fear and anger at her husband, she also felt guilty about having him arrested. She knew that the arrest would affect his career, and she did not want to bring shame or dishonor to him. Because of her worry about his status at work, she wanted to drop charges if he would agree to leave the household. He was released the following day. The police accompanied him back home to pick up his belongings, and he moved into an apartment in the neighboring town.

The mother reported that her husband had contacted a lawyer to begin separation proceedings and requested visitation with the children. Meanwhile, she had talked to the children about what had happened. She was surprised to learn from the children that they had heard their parents fighting for the past year or so, and that they were terrified of their father. They had no interest in seeing him. At that point, she hired an attorney and the case went to court.

The next step in this evaluation involved direct interviews with the children. I decided to interview them separately. I knew that this approach would be more stressful for the children, but I wanted to give each of them the chance to tell the story from his or her perspective and to do so in private. I interviewed Jenna first. She was a mature and verbal nine-year-old. She came calmly into the office, sat across from me, and looked directly at me. I asked her some initial questions about school, her favorite subjects and television shows. This preamble was both to put her at ease and to assess her mood and communication skills. She did not want to color or draw, but wished to get to the point of the interview. I asked her what she had been told about why she was here. She replied that she knew that I was the person who would tell the judge whether she should see her father, and she wanted to let me know that she did not want to see her father "ever again." As I asked Jenna to tell me more about this decision, she explained to me that her father and mother had been fighting for as long as she could remember. She fell asleep every night to the sounds of their fighting. When I asked her about what the worst part of the fighting was, her voice dropped and she said that she was afraid her mother would get killed. This was the first sign of emotion from this calm and mature little girl. I then asked her to tell me about the fight to which the police had responded. Again, her facial expression changed. She sat forward in her chair and began to fiddle with the papers in front of her. For the first time, she looked away as she began to talk. Soon, she had forgotten I was there and was reliving the fight.

She was waiting to go to school when the fight began, sitting in the living room, which was next to the kitchen. From where she sat, she had seen everything. She saw her parents yelling and saw her father grab her mother. He then turned and picked up a "big knife." "I thought he was going to cut her throat," she said. Her mother began to scream at the children to call the police. Her father yelled to Jenna, "If you call the police, I'll beat you." Jenna described being frozen with fear and indecision. In a panic she had run out of the house. As Jenna concluded the story, she burst into tears and sobbed uncontrollably. I gave her Kleenex, and when she had regained her composure, I asked her what the worst part of this experience had been for her. She cried quietly and said, "I left my mom. I was too scared he would hurt me and I couldn't call the police."

The response was heartbreaking. This brave and frightened girl was wrenched with guilt over her perceived failure to protect her mother. As we discussed this episode further, the depth of her shame and self-blame were striking. She replayed the event over and over in her head, she said, to try to figure out why she had "run away." The fact that her father had made a direct threat to her safety wasn't enough to assuage her guilt. In her eyes, she had failed her mother.

When I asked about her ideas for current visits, she again said that she had no interest in seeing her father. She said that the house was peaceful now, and she didn't care if he ever came back. While I doubted that her emotional reactions to her father were quite that simple, I was struck with how adamantly she reacted to the idea of visits.

My final interview was with seven-year-old Ben. As I would have predicted with someone his age, he was less verbal and had a shorter attention span. Instead of one longer interview, I decided to interview him twice for shorter periods of time. In the first interview, he seemed very nervous, fidgeting in his seat and avoiding eye contact. He declined the offer to draw a picture. I asked about what his understanding was of our visits, and he said that it was to decide about seeing his father. I asked why his parents were separated. He said that they fought a lot. I asked if he could tell me about the scariest fight, and he began to talk about the time the police had come.

His description was somewhat different from his sister's, both because of his age and because he had actually seen little. As he told the story, he was upstairs playing in his room when he heard shouting and arguing downstairs. He stayed in his room because he did not like the sounds of what he was hearing. Then he heard his mom screaming to call the police. He got "very scared" and thought about what he had learned at the school about calling 911. He placed the call. He could hear his father yelling. He said that he was so scared that he went back into his room, barricaded the door, and hid in the closet. I asked what he was most afraid of. He replied that he thought his father would hurt him. The police found him in his closet a short while later. As Ben told this story, he looked more and more anxious. He stopped talking and asked if he could leave the room. I commented that it must have been very scary for him and that he didn't have to talk about it any more if he didn't want to. He appeared to be visibly relieved and sank back in his chair. He then asked if he could draw a picture. His picture was of a cat "with blood all over his face." He declined to tell me more about the picture.

In the second interview, he was more relaxed and talked about school. He didn't have many positive things to say about school: He didn't like his teacher; he got into trouble for fighting, but it wasn't really his fault. I asked what he missed with his dad not being home. He said his dad used to play baseball with him and he missed that. When I asked Ben what he thought was important to think about if he was to have visits with his dad, he was quiet for a long time and then replied, "Well I think maybe we could have visits, but not for a long time." I asked about how long would be good. "When I am old enough to get away if I have to," Ben responded.

This case went to court with my recommendation that visits be postponed for the next six months until these children had been able to see a therapist and resolve some of their initial reactions to the violence they had witnessed.

As I thought about this case, one of the truths that emerged was the hidden nature of this family's life in an affluent suburb. I began to think about the ways in which class and privilege become their own forms of prison. It turned out that this mother had previously gone to the police about her husband's abusiveness. The police had offered her legal remedies and counseling. She had declined, however, explaining to me that she did not want to ruin her husband's reputation. All she wanted, she said, was an end to the abuse. She had no desire to embarrass him or jeopardize his job. The public nature of seeking a restraining order or having him arrested was humiliating, and she wanted to avoid this loss of privacy. It wasn't until she feared for her life that she decided to act. Even then, she declined a full restraining order, opting instead for a milder order that he stay away from the home. She wanted to help her husband save face.

Similarly, the children's needs went unrecognized. I talked with both teachers to get information about their functioning in school. Jenna, as I could have predicted, was an excellent student and a leader in the classroom. The teacher, who spoke with great affection about Jenna, was surprised to hear from the mother that the parents had separated. Ben's teacher gave a more mixed report. Ben was quite aggressive at times and had trouble focusing on his work. He seemed preoccupied with fighting, bringing action figures of wrestlers to school and engaging in pretend battles with them in the classroom. In fact, the teachers had recommended a learning evaluation for him. Not unexpectedly, the mother did not tell either teacher about the abuse. She didn't want anyone at school to know. Although one can readily understand the mother's reticence to confide in the teachers, it ultimately made their job more difficult, and limited their abilities to help the children. I could imagine that Jenna's teacher could have been an important refuge for Jenna if she had known. Jenna desperately needed to talk with someone about what was going on in her parents' home. The secrecy resulted in Jenna's feeling more singularly responsible for the situation. If Ben's teacher had received more complete information, she could have understood his aggressive behavior and his short attention span in a different light.

Another lesson from this family's story is about how differently children react to an event. This abuse had very distinct meanings for Jenna and Ben, and they showed their reactions in different ways. Jenna assumed responsibility for protecting her mother, and her mother's injuries were visible symbols of failure. I speculate that this assumption of responsibility was Jenna's because she was the oldest child. She was bright, verbal, and mature. These attributes made her both vulnerable and strong: vulnerable because she was burdened with expectations she could not fulfill; strong because these attributes helped her cope with the stress at home. Jenna is doing well in school. I hope that her intellect and engaging personality will continue to benefit her.

Ben, on the other hand, appears to be more vulnerable. Perhaps this is because of age (boys at this age usually lag behind girls in cognitive and social development), and because of gender (the role model of a father who is abusive presents complications for

Ben in his own development). Ben has already been identified in school as a troublemaker. He is both intrigued with aggression and frightened by its consequences. Perhaps his fascination is an attempt to neutralize his fear.

Both children have been affected in ways that their parents do not fully understand. The stigma of domestic violence in this comfortable community makes it difficult for anyone to talk openly about these occurrences.

CARMEN, ANNA, AND BILLY

Carmen, a twenty-five-year-old mother of two children—Anna, age five, and Billy, age three—was referred to the Child Witness to Violence Project by the children's pediatrician because he was concerned about their behavior. In a health visit, Carmen had told him that Billy was impossible to manage and that she was worried that he might get hurt. As an example of his behavior, Carmen reported an occasion when Billy got out of his bed at night and left their apartment. Fortunately, Carmen had heard him open the door and stopped him immediately. She was quite worried, however, that he might try to leave again. They live in an urban neighborhood that Carmen described as unsafe. His day care provider was also frustrated with him because he hit other children and would not heed limits in school. When the doctor asked about stresses at home that might be contributing to Billy's behavior, Carmen confided that she had obtained a restraining order from the court for protection against her abusive husband. The pediatrician was surprised; despite the fact that he had cared for the children since their birth, he had not known about these family problems. As he asked about the abuse, Carmen told him that it had been severe at times. She then pulled up her skirt to show scars on her legs from cigarette burns, inflicted by her husband. The doctor told her about the Child Witness to Violence Project and made a referral.

At the Project, as we discussed the referral in our team meeting, we decided that this case was urgent. The mother had been seriously abused. The three-year-old child was behaving in ways that were dangerous to himself, and we worried that this mother might not be able to keep him safe. One of the counselors called Carmen to set up an initial evaluation. Despite her apparent interest in coming to see the counselor, she failed to keep the appointment. The counselor called her back, this time spending more time with her on the telephone to assess the level of crisis. She found out that Carmen had been a victim of abuse for the past three years and that the children had witnessed numerous episodes of violence, including one instance of rape. It was this horrifying event that had propelled Carmen to go to court to seek protection. However, even after a restraining order was issued, her husband continued to come to the neighborhood. He was frequently seen outside their house. One morning, Carmen discovered that someone had broken into her basement; she suspected her husband. She called the police each time she or the children saw him; however, he would flee before the police arrived, thus avoiding arrest. Carmen also stated that she had little money and could not afford to move. In fact, she barely had enough money to feed and clothe her children. She had depended on her husband's income. Without it, she was desperate. Again, the counselor scheduled an appointment for Carmen to bring the children to our program. Carmen did not keep this appointment.

This pattern of making appointments and failing to keep them lasted for several weeks. We were very worried about the situation and struggled as a team to decide whether or not we should notify the state children's protective services about our safety concerns for the children. However, more information about the family emerged as the counselor continued to talk with Carmen on the telephone, convincing us to hold off on notifying children's protective services. First, Carmen told the counselor that she had gone to stay with her mother in another part of the city. She believed that she was safe. There were other adults in the home, and she would not be at this home alone. Second, Carmen confided that she had been in foster care as a child because her father was abusive to her. She hated the system and felt that it had created many more problems for her than it had solved. Because of her time in this system, she refused to consider a battered women's shelter as an option for safety. She told the counselor that she had lived in group homes before and felt that they were terrible places for children. Her worst fear was that her children would eventually be removed from her care and put into the foster care system. Ironically, Carmen believed that keeping herself and her children out of a shelter was the best way to ensure their safety. This fear also kept Carmen from bringing her children to see us.

The counselor explained her dilemma to Carmen: If she could not meet the children and get some sense of their well-being, she would be legally mandated to notify children's protective services. The counselor assured Carmen that she understood her fears and that as a program, we were dedicated to helping mothers establish safe environments for their children. The counselor's patience and respect for Carmen, along with her genuine empathy for Carmen's dilemma, paid off: Carmen brought her children in for an evaluation approximately three weeks after the first call to the program.

In the first interview Carmen was exhausted and overwhelmed. She had enrolled in a vocational training program, and it was important to her that she finish so that she could get a job. However, she was forced to commute long hours from her mother's home, and the children were not faring well. Billy was in day care. The center director had communicated her concern about his behavior, along with the warning that if things did not improve, Billy would be asked to leave. The day care staff worried that they could not protect the other children from Billy's aggression. Carmen thought about going to a shelter, but decided against it. In addition to her memories of her own shelter experiences, a move to a shelter would result in losing the day care slot for Billy.

The counselor interviewed both children. Billy was very active and unfocused in the session, running from one toy to another, but not able to engage with any specific activity. He said to the counselor that his dad hit his mom, but that she would be OK because he would protect her. When the counselor asked how he would do so, he replied that he had a knife. Anna, the five-year-old girl, was subdued and shy. She sat quietly in the room as the counselor talked with the mother. When she was interviewed alone, she was at first reluctant to talk. Her mother had said that Anna had trouble sleeping at night. The counselor began with that topic, asking Anna about nighttime. Anna replied that she was scared. When pressed to say more about her fears, Anna replied that she worried that her mother would die. She thought about this fear in school, and it made her sick to her stomach. She looked very sad as she talked about this fear. It was clear that she was suffering as much as Billy, only in a less obvious way.

Within three days of that interview, Carmen called to say that her husband had appeared at the school bus stop as she picked Anna up. She also said that Billy had climbed out the window of her second-story apartment early that morning. With this news, the counselor was convinced that the situation had deteriorated to a dangerous level and urged Carmen to take Billy to the local hospital's emergency room for a psychological evaluation. The counselor also told Carmen that she was so concerned about the children that she must notify children's protective services about the crisis. The counselor worried that Carmen would be angry and frightened and would cut off contact with everyone. Although Carmen told the counselor that she was angry and felt betrayed, she took Billy to the hospital, and he was admitted for an inpatient stay. The counselor made a report to the local children's protective services office, and an investigation began.

The counselor heard nothing from Carmen for the next three weeks. Finally, Carmen called to tell the counselor that although she had been very angry, she knew that the counselor was doing her best to help the family be safe. She agreed to come in again to talk. This exchange seemed to be crucial in helping Carmen accept help and commit to a relationship with the counselor. She and our counselor worked together for the next year. Progress was slow and erratic. Billy was released from the hospital and enrolled in a therapeutic day care program. His behavior improved dramatically. Carmen left her vocational training program, but later took pleasure in becoming a room parent at Billy's school. Children's protective services helped Carmen secure an apartment in another part of the city. This move was a great relief to everyone: They could now feel safer at home. As the initial crisis subsided, however, Carmen grew more depressed and immobilized. She began to confide in the counselor her own history of abuse, something she had never before discussed with anyone. Together, Carmen and her counselor decided that Carmen should be hospitalized to help manage her sense of hopelessness and desolation. This hospitalization was somewhat helpful for Carmen, but devastating for the children. Their fears and worries about their mother were vividly revived.

Anna continued to have significant difficulty in school. She was afraid of other children and began to fall behind in her work. She begged her mother to be allowed to stay at home. Carmen once commented that Anna seemed to prefer punishment to going to school. She developed chronic headaches and stomachaches. During one session with the counselor, Anna explained that she was particularly afraid to ride the bus to school. The counselor was curious about this fear. Anna told her that she had been struck by a ball that someone had tossed around the bus. In addition, a girl sitting near her had recently been hit with a rock that was thrown into the window by a person on the street. She also said that the bus was often late picking her up and that there were too many children on the bus. In short, Anna began each day by feeling scared and vulnerable. With her previous exposures to dangerous violence, Anna was highly sensitive and fearful about random or unexpected danger in her environment. It was no wonder she had trouble focusing on her work in school. The counselor helped the mother contact school officials about the bus situation. Although it finally improved, Anna lost most of that academic year in terms of achievement in school. Because she was quiet and caused little trouble, neither her teachers nor the school officials were aware of her distress.

At the end of fifteen months of counseling, Carmen and Billy were greatly improved. Anna was no longer afraid at school, although she continued to have academic difficulties. Stable and safe housing was perhaps the most important component of the family's improvement. High-quality day care made a dramatic difference for Billy. Carmen re-enrolled in the vocational program, which led to job placement. Throughout this time, the counselor continued to provide a steady, warm, and accepting relationship with Carmen and the children. She provided great stability throughout much of the initial crisis. Carmen articulated the value of this relationship in a letter she wrote to the counselor, thanking the counselor for caring about her family and believing that they could make it through the crises they had endured.

This case is a grim reminder of the intermingling effects of exposure to domestic violence and poverty. Unlike the first family, Carmen and her children lacked the basic necessities of safe housing. Carmen had no safety net of savings. She could barely feed her children. She had few friends and did not use community resources. For reasons that are quite different from those of the first family, Carmen also refused shelter. Her own history of abandonment and abuse made her distrustful of most people and institutions. Perhaps because she was poor and lived in a high-crime neighborhood, the police were also less responsive. They failed to apprehend her husband, thus making it possible for him to continue a reign of terror over the family. In short, neither the legal nor the community support system worked for Carmen. What began as a problem between Carmen and her husband grew to include each family member. Anna, who was perhaps most seriously affected by the violence, displayed the least obvious symptoms and therefore initially did not get the help she needed. The schools were particularly unresponsive to Anna's needs.

These cases illustrate both the immediate and long-lasting effects of exposure to domestic violence on children. We see that children are affected in unique ways that depend partially on their personalities, their strengths, their ages, and their relationships with their parents. We can also understand how the effects of chronic trauma on adults affect their capacities to parent their children. Carmen's extensive history of abuse affected her ability to make good judgments about keeping her children safe. It wasn't until she began to recognize the severity of her own trauma that she could improve her parenting relationships with her children.

These cases also raise complex intervention and policy questions. In the case of Ben and Jenna, the question of what contact they should have with their father is unresolved. How does the court balance the children's rights to feel safe with the right of a parent to have access to his children? How does the court weigh the importance of children maintaining an ongoing connection with both parents with the need of the mother to be free from her abusive husband? In the second case, the counselor struggled with the definition of child abuse or neglect. Is it abusive or neglectful on the part of parents to physically hurt one another in front of the children? Who should be charged with the neglect in this case: the father for his terrifying and dangerous behavior or the mother for her failure to protect the children? There are no easy answers to these questions.

In conclusion, the problems that face children and women affected by domestic violence are complex. The particular horror of domestic violence for children is that it robs them of the basic sense of home as a safe haven. They learn at an early age that it may not be safe to depend on adult caregivers for refuge. These lessons are learned behind closed doors, away from the eyes or ears of the community. The adult victim and the perpetrator of the violence each has his or her own reasons for keeping the silence. A complex interplay of fear of escalating violence, economic dependence, as well as fear of judgment and shame keep the victim quiet. Fear of sanction and the need for control silence the perpetrator. In order to create interventions that help in these situations, we must create a social climate that breaks the code of silence and brings the devastating phenomenon of domestic violence into the public light.

CHAPTER 4

What We Can Do to Help Children Who Have Witnessed Violence

The first chapters of this book are sobering. Children are profoundly affected by violence in their environments. There seems to be no age at which a child is immune to the effects of exposure to violence. Exposure to domestic violence, the kind of violence that is most private and difficult to acknowledge, seems to be particularly harmful to children. In the face of the evidence, many of us begin to despair. What can we do to help children? How can we raise awareness and begin to think as parents and professionals about prevention? These next three chapters focus on these questions.

When we provide training to professionals about the effects of violence on young children, we always allow time for questions and reflections. We solicit questions from the audience and there is usually silence. People's expressions are drawn. Sometimes, a person may be in tears. Frequently, someone will take this opportunity to say that he or she has personal experience with the issue. We hear these stories no matter where we are: a large city, a small suburban town, a rural area. Our audiences tell us that it is hard to hear this information about children because it makes their work seem futile. How could they possibly help? What could they do to make a difference? We are quick to stress that just as we have learned about how violence affects children, we have also learned that there is a great deal we can do to help them.

CHILDREN'S VOICES ABOUT WHAT HELPS

In interviews with children, we frequently ask what they do to help themselves when they are frightened, or whether or not they have someone they can talk to when they are scared. They tell us that talking about frightening memories is helpful. When asked whether counseling helped, one little boy said, "It's like the counselor takes the thoughts out of my head. Then I feel better." This description conveys the magical thinking of a seven-year-old who wishes to banish the bad thoughts forever. However, it also gives us a clue about the relief this child feels that he can share these bad thoughts with an adult. They no longer belong to him. They are shared with the counselor. In another session, a girl is asked about her drawings. She has amassed many drawings of the street on which she witnessed a shooting. She draws various people and events in exquisite detail, using many colors. She talks with her counselor about what happens as she draws. "It's like the feelings come out on the tip of my marker." Again, we hear this girl's relief at being able to let go of the intense feelings that get stirred up in the face of trauma. This "letting go" takes place within the safety of a relationship with a trusted and caring adult.

One of our counselors once asked a child to draw a picture of what helped her cope with fear. She filled her paper with people and places, including her mother, her grandmother, her teacher, her church, and a police officer. She explained that these people helped her in different ways and that they were all important. This picture has come to represent our vision about who we must involve in the effort to help children affected by violence: parents, teachers, faith communities, and police officers. Each of these professionals, and others as well, have a role to play in helping children.

THE ROLE OF PARENTS IN HELPING CHILDREN EXPOSED TO VIOLENCE

Parents are the first resource for most children when they are frightened. The ability of parents to provide an emotional buffer for children under stress has been documented in countless ways.

Many studies show that children handle stress better when they are near their parents. They also show that it is better for children to remain with their parents, even in stressful situations (such as war), than to be separated from them.[1] Parents are enormously influential in the way a child interprets violence in the environment.

Cynthia Dickstein, a successful freelance writer, wrote about her experience of living with domestic violence as a child.[2] She chronicled the abuse she witnessed, her mother's slow decline into alcoholism and sexual promiscuity, her efforts to protect her mother, and her attempts to intercede in her parents' fighting. She also wrote of her complicated and ambivalent reactions to her parents. She was deeply ashamed of her mother and as a teenager worried that she would grow up to be like her. She idolized her father (and he, in turn, doted on his only daughter) and could not understand how someone who loved her so much could do something so wrong.

In an interview with Cynthia, I asked her about what had helped her cope with the horrors she lived with as a child. Without hesitating, she replied that there were two messages she got from her parents, even in the midst of their warring rage, that stayed with her. The first was that they both loved her deeply and were proud that she was smart and successful in school. The second message was that the fighting had nothing to do with her. She says, "I began at an early age to believe that the craziness in my house belonged to my parents, not to me; that the awful things they were doing, they were doing to each other, not to me; and that they were responsible, not me. They never blamed me and that made all the difference." Cynthia's experiences remind us that even when there is violence between parents, the way they interpret the experience for their children can make a difference.

Many parents we see have forgotten this basic truth. Because of their guilt or their sense of hopelessness they doubt their ability to help their children, or they underestimate the effectiveness of their relationships with their children. The story of the Jones family gives another testimony to the power of parents in children's lives.

THE JONES FAMILY

The Jones family, three children and their parents, sought the services of our program after hearing about us from the police. This family had experienced the unthinkable horror of seeing their son's best friend fatally shot in a random act of violence. The story they told was unforgettable: One summer day the children were on the porch of their house with several of their friends. Wayne, the sixteen-year-old son, had just gone into the house to get a snack when gunshots rang out. He rushed outside to see his best friend, Eric, staggering toward the house drenched in blood. Eric made it into the house and collapsed in the front hall. Wayne's father ran downstairs and tried to resuscitate him while Wayne called the police. Efforts to help Eric survive were futile. He was dead by the time the police arrived.

The family was in shock. The police referred them to the Child Witness to Violence Project and our staff saw them together a few days after the shooting. Disbelief and guilt dominated the first session. Wayne was convinced that his decision to go inside the house for food had somehow cost his friend his life. The logic was irrational, but the passions were real. If he had not been so self-centered as to want a snack, he could have pushed his friend out of the way. Perhaps the bullet was meant for him and by his leaving at that moment, his friend had died instead. Eric was popular and smart; he (Wayne) wasn't as responsible; somehow he should have been taken instead of Eric. His guilt was almost unbearable for the family (and the counselors) to tolerate.

The father's version of guilt and helplessness was focused on the fact that he had been unable to revive Eric. Again, the facts of the case meant little. Eric was shot in the heart with virtually no chance of survival. However, the father had previous training as a paramedic and felt that this training should have allowed him to save Eric. He reviewed every step of his intervention with the paramedics who arrived at the house. No amount of reassurance could convince him that Eric's death was not his fault.

The two younger sisters, ages five and eight, were terrified. They drew pictures of Eric lying in their hall. The striking feature of the pictures was the amount of blood: Red colored everywhere on the page. The mother cried for most of the first sessions. She could barely speak.

As we worked with this family, their reactions moved from disbelief and grief to anger. How could this have happened so suddenly to someone they loved? Who would be next? The parents discussed the possibility of sending the children to live with relatives in another state for the summer. They worried about their safety and doubted their ability to protect the children.

In one session, the children talked about the senseless acts of violence they saw daily. They talked about drugs and gangs on the street, and drive-by shootings. The father listened carefully and began to share his perspectives on racism and poverty. This man, who had been rather quiet and stoic in previous sessions, was passionate and eloquent as he laid out his argument. White people wanted black people to kill each other and poison each other with drugs. No one cared about people living in the inner city. Poor people, especially poor people of color, were beneath regard of the government and service providers. To buttress this argument, he cited a recent news article that focused on the death of a white suburban teenager who had been killed in a boating accident. The article mentioned that grief counselors had been available to help the boy's schoolmates and neighbors. "Where are the grief counselors in our neighborhood?" he wondered. "They don't care what happens to black teenagers."

As he talked, I observed the children. They were rapt with attention. I was aware of my own discomfort at being a white therapist. However, he was not angry at me personally. His explanation gave reason to this random and senseless act of violence. It provided a framework of logic for his children to grasp. It also provided a target for their anger. His persuasiveness and deep belief were ultimately reassuring for the children.

The family survived the tragedy. When we met for the final time, the children were back in school and the family was struggling with the decision of whether to move out of the neighborhood to a safer area of the city. The strength of the parents, their ability to acknowledge and tolerate strong emotions, and ultimately their anger at the system gave support and sustenance to the children.

Parents are the most important frontline supporters of their children. By their ability to listen, to help children understand, to interpret the world for children, and to provide an emotional buffer, they help children withstand the most traumatic events. When we see parents in the Child Witness to Violence Project, we explicitly reassure them that even though there was little they could have done to prevent their child's exposure to trauma, there is a great deal they can do to help their child regain a sense of equilibrium. We suggest that parents focus on three areas with their children.

The first task is to help children reestablish a sense of order and routine. Children have a greater need for routine and predictability after a traumatic event has shattered their world. We suggest that parents take extra care at bedtime to be with their child, read a story, or participate in some kind of activity that will soothe and reassure the child. Parents may spend extra time with their child to explain what will happen each day so that the child can anticipate activities and transitions. Since many children, especially young children, will be anxious about separations from parents, absences should be talked about ahead of time and carefully explained to children.

A second task for parents is to provide careful explanations of the violent events. The explanation should be appropriate to the child's developmental stage and should contain only as much information as is necessary. The first goal of the explanation is to help children, who may be self-centered in their thinking, to understand that the violence is not their fault. The second goal is to communicate the message that this is a subject that can be talked about. As we will see in the case of Jacob and his grandmother, mentioned later in this chapter, talking about a traumatic event may be difficult for adults, but is clearly important for children.

A third goal for parents is to respond to children's fears and worries honestly and with whatever reassurance is possible. Part of the helplessness parents feel is that they are often unable to provide any guarantees for the safety of their children. This is particularly true for parents who live in chronically dangerous communities. Children need to hear that we, as adults, are doing everything we can to make the world safe for our children. This declaration is quite reassuring for young children, even though we, as adults, know that there are limits to what we can accomplish.

THE ROLE OF PSYCHOTHERAPY FOR CHILDREN AND FAMILIES

We received a call several years ago from a mother who wondered if she should bring her child in to see us. She had read about our program in the local newspaper. She told us that her eight-year-old son, Andrew, had developed an intense fear that he would be kidnapped and that this fear was starting to "control his life," as she described it. She told me that Andrew had seen a program on television about the kidnapping and eventual murder of Polly Klaas, a twelve-year-old girl from California who was abducted from her bedroom and never seen again. This incident, which received considerable national publicity, was horrifying, touching adults' and children's most primitive worries about keeping children safe. If a child isn't safe in her own bedroom, how is it possible to assure safety anywhere? This mother described how Andrew wasn't able to go to sleep at night and felt comfortable only if he slept in his parents' bedroom. His sleep problems had begun to wear on everyone's nerves and she wondered what she should do. I suggested that she bring Andrew in so that we could talk.

In the first session with Andrew, he readily admitted that he was scared and that he could not get the worries about being kidnapped out of his head. It wasn't a problem during the day; however, at night, he was really frightened. He explained to me, with all the logic of an eight-year-old, that since Polly Klaas had been snatched from her bedroom, how could he not worry that the same thing would happen to him? I also learned that the family had recently moved to a new house in a new neighborhood. This house had large sliding glass doors along the back. Andrew's bedroom was adjacent to the sliding doors. Andrew told me that his specific worry was that someone would come into the house via the sliding doors and his parents would not know it because they slept at the other end of the house. After some discussion, his mother and he decided to move his room temporarily, so that he was farther away from the doors. He was considerably reassured by this solution because "if the kidnappers come now my parents will see them first." This simple intervention tells us about the benefits of counseling and about the almost magical beliefs that children have about the invincibility of their parents.

For many children who witness traumatic violence or injury to others, both their and their caregivers' capacities to cope may be overwhelmed. Despite the most sensitive efforts and responses of adults, the stress is too much, and outside help is needed. It is sometimes difficult for parents to decide when a child might need therapy, and whom to turn to for help. In our work with parents, we ask them to think about three things in deciding whether to seek professional help. First, we want to know about the changes in behavior or functioning the child is experiencing and how long the child has experienced the symptoms. We remind parents that many short-term symptoms of trauma, such as sleep difficulties, repeated thoughts or worries about the incident, increased worries about the safety of loved ones, or the development of new fears, are normal responses to an abnormal event. We urge parents to give their children extra time and availability, to allow their children to talk about their worries, to actively talk with them about how they can feel safe again. If the symptoms are short-lived, there may be no need for counseling. However, if they are persistent or interfere with the child's day-to-day life, then counseling may be helpful. In Andrew's case, although the symptoms were relatively mild and contained, the stress of his nighttime fears was affecting the entire family. In this case brief outside help made a big difference.

A second aspect to consider is the severity of the violence that the child witnessed. If the victim was a caregiver or a close family member, or if the violence was especially horrific, counseling may be indicated. Finally, if the child is in a situation of ongoing risk, or if the parent is unable to care for the child adequately, the child should be referred for therapy.

What to Expect from Therapy

When we provide counseling services to a child in our program, we usually begin the first session by meeting with the child and parent(s) together. We wish to hear from everyone about what happened and the reasons they are seeking help. In addition to the important information we gather, we find that these first sessions are important in setting a tone for the work we will do together. Many children are uncertain about whether it is permissible to talk about violence they have witnessed, particularly if the violence occurred within their home. An open discussion about the violence gives important messages to children that it is OK to talk about these difficult subjects. If their parents talk about it to the counselor, then it frees the child to talk after the parent has left the room. Sometimes we may specifically ask the parent if it is permissible for us to talk with a child about the violence after the parent has left.

After the ground rules are established, we usually meet with the child alone to begin to understand the problems from his or her perspective. We see children in a well-equipped playroom that contains a variety of toys, art materials, books, puppets, and dress-up clothes, all available to help children express themselves in the ways that seem most comfortable. Some children prefer to play rather than talk, and will tell us about themselves through dramatic play. Others like to draw pictures. Some read books or make up stories. One of our most important guiding principles is to support the child's pace and tolerance for talking about difficult subjects. Some children begin to tell us about the violence in their lives before we even ask. Others are very reluctant to talk or actively avoid any mention of the topic. We do not think it is appropriate or helpful to push a child to talk before he or she is ready. For some children, the emotions are too raw and fragile and they must avoid reminders of the frightening memories. With these children, we follow their lead in talking or in playing with toys of their choosing.

For many children, the power of the trauma in their lives is impossible to suppress, even if they are actively avoiding talking about it. It usually doesn't take long before a reference to the unmentionable events is made, either in play or in words. I once evaluated a four-year-old girl who was referred by her day care provider after she told the provider her father had pushed her mother "so hard that she fell down." The teacher suggested to the mother that she seek help from our program. When I met with Ruth and her mother together, the mother said that she and her husband fought frequently. In addition to this most recent episode in which her husband had lost control, the mother described that mealtimes were frequently marred by arguing. Her husband sometimes threw dishes or refused to speak at the table. She expressed concern about how the children would be affected by this constant tension in the house. Ruth sat quietly as her mother talked. She looked very sad, avoiding eye contact with her mother or me. When the mother left the room, I commented that it sounded as if things were sometimes scary at home. Ruth disagreed by saying that actually, things were OK. I mentioned that her mother had been talking about the fights between the parents. Ruth said, "Oh, no! My parents don't fight." I began to realize that Ruth could not tolerate this subject and that she was telling me that we could not talk about it. So, I changed the subject, asking her if she might draw a picture of her family, so I could know who they were. She looked relieved and went to get markers from the shelf. With great focus, Ruth began to draw a picture of a large house. The house filled the paper. On either side of the house, she drew two small figures. I asked her about the drawing. With few words, she told me that the figures on one side of the house were her mother and herself; on the other side of the house were her father and her younger brother. I asked why they were outside the house. She quickly replied, "Because they will fight if they are inside the house." With this declaration, Ruth seemed to be allowing me to ask more questions about the figures on the paper. Careful to phrase my questions in an impersonal way, I asked why these people were fighting and what happened during the fights. By talking about the figures on the paper Ruth began to communicate her experiences in her family.

The aim of therapy for children is generally to help them reestablish psychological equilibrium after a traumatic event. For many children, the opportunity to talk with a professional in the context of a safe relationship and therapeutic space is very helpful. This is especially true for children who witness domestic violence. These children are often caught in the middle of angry and contentious fighting between parents. They have additional need for the safe and neutral space that therapy offers. The child may review the violence with the counselor, but doing so in a safe space offers the child a chance to master feelings of terror, guilt, and anxiety. A counselor who can reflect on the experience with a child offers a perspective that can relieve the child's fear or worry. Some therapists use relaxation techniques to help children regain the ability to calm themselves. Children who are severely traumatized may benefit from medication to diminish anxiety symptoms.

Because two of the most typical symptoms of traumatic exposure to violence are impulsive behavior and high levels of activity, some professionals are concerned that traumatic stress reactions may be confused with the diagnosis of attention deficit/hyperactivity disorder in children. Children are then placed on medication that is inappropriate and ineffective. In fact, the exact diagnosis can be a challenge for medical providers. Experts agree that it is essential that the physician obtain a thorough history of any trauma the child may have experienced, as well as detailed information from the parents and teachers about the behavior problems.[3] It is also important that parents feel that they can communicate openly with the treating physician and that the doctor is willing to listen to their perspectives on their child.

In addition to providing help for the child, the therapist should work with the parents to discuss the child's progress and strategies to help stabilize the child. Ideally, the parents and the therapist function as a team to reestablish a feeling of safety for the child. Working as a team becomes more difficult, however, when the violence is domestic violence. Working with an abusive parent is complicated; it can also make the situation at home more difficult and even dangerous for the family. Abusing parents do not want their secrets to be told. They fear the involvement of children's protective services or law enforcement. They may become angry if other family members talk about what is happening at home. In our project, unless the abuser has been required to confront the abuse through the legal system, we work only with the non-abusing parent and children. If an abuser's behavior is recognized by the legal system, it is no longer a secret.

Sometimes, parents need assistance in making sense of the symptoms that a child displays. Helping parents understand that these symptoms are often a response to fear can be reassuring to them. The therapist and parents may work together to devise strategies to deal with certain behaviors in a child, such as exaggerated fears of nighttime or reluctance to separate from a parent during the day. Finally, parents need reassurance and support in their efforts to help their children.

THE ROLE OF TEACHERS

In nearly every seminar we offer to teachers about this topic, we hear a story about one of their students who has had direct experience with violence. Our seminars draw a broad range of teachers from many different settings. However, their stories are remarkably similar: Jimmy, age three, announces in circle time that he saw someone getting hurt on the street. Maria, age six, says in school that her parents fight and that her dad pushed her mother down the stairs. After hearing about the shootings at Columbine High School in Littleton, Colorado, Hal, age six, worries that it will happen in his school and is scared to go out on the playground. Rebecca, age four, plays a game in the housekeeping corner at preschool. In the game, she yells at the dolls for fighting and then she hits them. We believe that teachers see and hear more of these stories than any other caregivers of children besides parents.

Teachers wonder how to respond to these children. Should

they be allowed to talk about violent incidents in the classroom? Should they be allowed to play out what they have seen, or does this scare other children? As teachers face these dilemmas, they describe an increasing sense of helplessness about the amount of violence that children live with. They feel inadequate to the task; they resent that they cannot teach these children because they are too distracted and preoccupied to learn; they receive inadequate support from school systems that measure learning only by standardized test scores. It is ironic that the professionals who spend the most time with children often feel the least prepared to work with children who live with chronic violence.

Children who live with violence bring their worries and fears into the classroom. The worries are reflected in their behavior, in anxiety about the safety of their parents or family members, in difficulties with concentration, and in poor social interactions with other children. They may be impulsive, distractible, or withdrawn. They are difficult to teach and sometimes remind teachers of their own weaknesses. They need stable adults in their lives, but their behavior often pushes these adults away. Sometimes teachers inadvertently communicate to their students that they do not want to hear about this part of students' lives.

Huy Tran and His Picture

One of our staff members observed the following interaction between a teacher and a student in a second-grade classroom. In observance of Veterans Day, the class was asked to write letters or draw pictures to soldiers to thank them for keeping our country safe. In her preparatory lesson for this activity, the teacher emphasized the important role of the military and stressed that soldiers were unrecognized and unappreciated by most people, especially in peacetime. When the children finished their task, they were asked to say a few words about their projects. Each child read or described his or her drawing. Most sounded similar, with many thank-yous and some portrayals of soldiers as brave and strong. One picture stood out, however. Huy Tran, a Vietnamese child, drew a picture of soldiers killing people. It was a jumbled and chaotic picture, with red blood on each person. He talked about the picture in a dispassionate tone, simply stating that it was about soldiers who fought in a war. A closer look at the picture showed a dismembered body in the lower corner. The teacher made no comment to the class. However, afterward, when she was talking with our staff person, she expressed irritation that Huy Tran had failed at this task. She described him as an "odd child" and stated that he didn't seem to want to learn in school. The staff person wondered aloud about the meaning of the picture, but the teacher dismissed it as another example of his failure to follow directions.

We discussed this incident and wondered about Huy Tran's family. Because we work with many Vietnamese families, we know of their histories of trauma associated with the prolonged conflict and subsequent dislocation of families in the Vietnam War. Some of the parents we work with have been victims of torture or have seen family members killed. They have spent years in refugee camps before immigrating to the United States. We wondered if Huy Tran's picture was an accurate reflection of his reality concerning soldiers and war. We also worried that his perspective was not validated by his teacher, who saw his picture only as an act of disobedience.

There is a great deal that teachers can do to help children who have violence in their lives. The capacity to form warm, secure relationships comes naturally for most teachers. Children, particularly young children, generally idolize their teachers, so the words of a teacher are quite powerful. Teachers can be good listeners and can encourage children to share their worries and fears in the classroom. For example, Huy Tran's teacher missed a unique opportunity to learn about his life. She could have asked him to talk about his picture or about his experiences with soldiers or war. She could also have asked about his family. Sometimes teachers may be afraid to dwell on difficult or frightening subjects in the classroom, for fear of upsetting other children. This is a legitimate concern. However, experienced teachers are able to assess when children are becoming anxious about a subject, and can redirect a child's conversation while making a mental note to talk with that child privately.

The ability to create classrooms that are safe, predictable, and comfortable is also second nature to many teachers. These children need to know what to expect each day. They react to a teacher's absence, a visitor in the classroom, or a change in the routine. It is important for teachers to realize that children who live with chaos benefit strongly from classrooms that are well organized and structured. In our work with vulnerable children and families, we have seen dramatic changes in children after they are placed in a supportive and structured school environment. Their anxieties decrease; their behavior improves. They begin to experience success and affirmation in a classroom setting, experiences that they may not have had previously.

Hillary and Her Grandfather

The story of Hillary illustrates the skills of teachers in helping children cope with fear. A few years ago, we received a distraught telephone call from a local preschool teacher for consultation about a child in her class. This was an experienced teacher whom we knew well. The subject of her call was Hillary, a four-year-old whose behavior had changed drastically over the past three weeks. Hillary, who had been an outgoing and happy child, was now withdrawn, clingy, and anxious. She could not sleep at naptime. Her mother was similarly concerned about her behavior, reporting that she was having nightmares and was unhappy about coming to school in the morning. When we asked about any changes or difficulties in Hillary's household, the teacher knew of nothing. However, she remembered that Hillary's grandfather had committed suicide a year ago by hanging himself in the family garage. The grandfather had lived in another town. Hilary's mom had been careful to protect her (then age three) from talk about what had happened to her grandfather; Hillary had not gone to the funeral.

At the time, Hillary spoke little about the death and seemed unaffected by this loss. The teacher's hunch was that something was worrying or frightening her, but that she didn't want to talk about it. This teacher knew Hillary and her mom well. After discussing the case with us, the teacher decided to be quite direct with Hillary by sharing with her the concern that something was worrying her that she was not talking about. She would then instruct Hillary to dictate a letter that would explain what she worried about. (My colleague and I thought that this strategy might be a bit unorthodox, and we worried about putting pressure on Hillary. However, we also knew this teacher very well and respected her skills with children.) A couple days later, the teacher called us with an interesting report. As instructed, Hillary wrote the letter. She directed it to her grandfather and told him that she could not go to sleep at night because she thought that he would come to her with a rope around his neck and that his head might fall off. She said that she was scared to close her eyes. When the teacher talked to Hillary about the letter, the reason for her behavior became evident. Hillary said that she had heard people talking about her grandfather and that she had recently seen a scary movie at a babysitter's house where a man was hanged. His ghost came back to haunt people.

The teacher went on to ask Hillary what she remembered about her grandfather. Hillary shared some pleasant memories about being in a park on a swing with her grandfather. But she repeated her worry about the fact that he had hanged himself. It was obvious that she had heard details of his death and did not fully understand them. The teacher suggested that they talk with the mother about this. As she suspected, the mother was shocked to hear that Hillary knew a great deal about her grandfather's death. Suddenly, it became clear to everyone: Because this was the anniversary of his death, Hillary had again heard people talking about him. Simultaneously, she had seen a frightening and inappropriate movie with her babysitter (which the mother did not know about). Her behavior, fears, and anxieties were completely understandable in this context.

The teacher's interventions were ideal. She made time in the day to take Hillary aside. She relied on her close relationship with

Hillary to encourage her to talk about what was bothering her. It was evident that Hillary trusted her teacher and felt comfortable talking with her. The teacher became an active advocate to help her feel better by involving her mother. And she was successful. Hillary's symptoms began to decrease immediately. When we called for a follow-up consultation with this teacher, we were quick to point out that this intervention had taken place without a mental health provider. It was decided that Hillary was doing much better and there was no need for follow-up counseling.

Effective Support for Teachers

One of the most frequent complaints we hear from teachers is that their training does not include information about how to work effectively with children who have witnessed violence. In fact, with the current national preoccupation about mandatory testing for children, teachers feel that there is even less emphasis on the social and emotional development of children and on strategies for helping vulnerable children. We believe that teachers must receive training and consistent supervisory support in order to adequately help children who live with violence. Training should include information about child development and the effects of exposure to violence on children of different ages. It should include an overview of the dynamics of domestic violence as well as information about children and media violence. It should emphasize practical problem-solving strategies. How should a teacher respond if a child announces to the class that he has seen a murder? What should a teacher do if a child draws a picture of her parents fighting? Training should remind teachers that not all children react in the same way and that some children are able to use the support and stability that school offers to withstand the effects of trauma. Finally, teachers need support to look at their own reactions to and experiences with violence. Teachers, like any other professionals, may live with personal experiences of violence, and this affects their work with children. For example, one teacher whose classroom I observed told me that she had grown up with parents who were abusive to each other and to her. When she discovered that a child in her room lived with chronic domestic violence, she was very vocal in her criticism of the mother for allowing her daughter to be exposed to such violence. In her discussion with me, she realized that her anger was intensified because of her own experiences, and that it was really directed at her own parents for what they had put her through. Teachers need a forum to consider the emotional impact of their work on their own lives. Too often, teachers are given neither the time nor permission to engage in this type of self-reflection.

FIRST RESPONDERS: THE ROLE OF POLICE OFFICERS

In our initial discussions about the need for the Child Witness to Violence Project, one of the first challenges we faced was identifying children who might benefit from our services. How would we find them? Unlike direct victims of violence, they would not have obvious injuries, and they were not likely to come to the hospital to request counseling services. As we discussed this problem, it occurred to us that perhaps we could use the police as case finders and promoters of the program. After all, police were often the first on the scene of a violent event, and they were in an important position to see children who had witnessed traumatic violence. In fact, they might see a large group of children and families affected by violence that we would not see at the hospital. As I pondered a collaboration with the police department, it occurred to me that I had worked with high-risk families for most of my professional life, yet had rarely worked with police officers. I had not given them much thought, and did not consider them one of the resources I might use to help families I worked with. For me, the police operated in another sphere, one that I actually knew little about.

With some trepidation we approached the Boston Police Department about this idea of collaboration. I assumed that our program was so far afield from law enforcement issues that we might not be taken seriously. However, I was completely wrong. The command staff we spoke to welcomed us. They told story after story about children they saw in the course of responding to calls for assistance. They talked about responding to domestic violence calls and seeing children huddled in the corner of an apartment. They told of their extreme discomfort at securing the scene of a murder and having children standing there, staring at the victim. A consistent theme underlay these stories. The police saw the children but did not know what to do for them. As one officer said, "We know how to secure a crime scene, but we have no idea what to do for the children." Consequently, they usually did nothing.

This failure to intervene with children worried the officers we spoke with. They knew that these kids were at risk. They wondered if this type of exposure to violence would make the kids behave violently themselves. They sometimes felt guilty leaving the children in dangerous or unresponsive environments. However, they did not know what else to do. So they were delighted to have a concrete resource to offer kids and families. Thus began a referral partnership that has been a cornerstone of the Child Witness to Violence Project since our early days.

A short time after this initial meeting with the police, the captain of one of the districts called and asked if we could provide training to his officers on effectively working with children, or on how to recognize their needs and respond to them in sensitive ways. This idea went beyond the simple task of referring children for counseling and began to consider the role of a police officer in helping a child feel safe. It was an intriguing idea that led to the establishment of a training seminar for police officers that we have offered regularly in the city of Boston for the past seven years. In these seminars, we teach basic principles of child development as they relate to policing. We use actual cases that police bring to discuss why children react to traumatic events in certain ways. We focus on how exposure to violence affects children, and how officers can respond sensitively to children's needs.

In the course of providing training to hundreds of officers on the subject of children who are exposed to violence, we have learned a great deal about how officers can help children and what children think about police officers. We strongly believe that police officers can be important models of positive authority in the lives of children, and that the way they interact with children during a time of crisis is important.

Police represent safety and predictability to many children. They are the most visible reminders of rules and societal order and that rules exist to keep people safe. When asked what police officers do, most young children respond simply, "They arrest people," or "They put bad guys in jail." This simplistic view of the role of police in society speaks partly to the developmental needs of young children for clear rules and expectations. It also speaks to their need for safety and reassurance.

This symbolic importance of a police officer's work was made clear to me when I worked with a young boy who had seen several shootings in his neighborhood, including one fatal shooting that occurred just outside his house. Eric's mother had brought him in because Eric was afraid to go to school, which was two blocks from his house. This response was not unexpected, given what Eric had witnessed. Eric was falling behind in school and his mother was exasperated and powerless to effect any change in his fears. Eric drew many pictures that depicted scenes of the "bad men" shooting guns. He was quite open with his fears, although he also felt ashamed of them. His vulnerability was palpable. In addition to allowing him the opportunity to talk about his feelings, we started to brainstorm with him and his mother about a practical strategy for helping him feel safe enough to get to school in the morning. He refused to have his mother walk him to school, this being in his eyes the ultimate public statement of weakness. We decided to contact the school to see if we could arrange for a bus to stop for him. This would be possible only if I wrote a letter, emphasizing the emotional vulnerabilities of this child and convincing the school that there were unmet mental health needs that transportation could address. Just as we were set to pursue this strategy, Eric came into my office one day and excitedly said, "I have figured out how to go to school!" He then told me that there was a police officer at the end of his street who stood there each morning because of a construction project. If he could see the police officer and walk by him, Eric was convinced that he would feel safe enough to resume his pattern of walking to school. Eric was emboldened to try this plan, and it worked. He was able to walk to school, tentatively at first, but then, with practice, he began to forget about his fears.

I was struck by the symbolic power of the officer, who was such a powerful presence in Eric's eyes. I was equally sure that this policeman had no idea how important he was to this boy. Even though we, as adults, knew that there were limits to this officer's ability to fully protect the neighborhood, Eric needed to believe that the officer was in charge.

In our training with police, we discuss situations that officers have responded to in which children were present. We stress the importance of officers being aware of children who are bystanders to violent events. We focus on how a child might understand or respond to the situation, how the officer can reassure the child, and what kinds of help the child and family may need after the crisis. In our work with police, we stress the importance of their roles with children. We encourage them to interact with children in benign situations (such as in schools and in the community) as often as possible, so that children see them as helpful and trustworthy resources and aren't afraid of them. The district we have worked with most closely has produced "cop cards," the police equivalent of baseball cards, for children to collect. There is a card for every officer, with information about his or her hobbies, favorite books, or other interests. While some critics dismissed this initiative as a waste of money, we at the Child Witness to Violence Project thought it was a brilliant strategy to normalize relationships between children and police officers. The children we saw were enthusiastic collectors of cards, and got to know several police officers in the process.

A colleague tells a story about his early memory of a police officer, which we use to begin each seminar series. James grew up in a household that was dominated by his father, whom he described as scary and unpredictable. His father routinely terrorized his mother; James remembers frequent fights that included physical abuse of his mother. One night he awoke to hear his mother screaming. She called the police, who arrived quickly. To his great relief, they arrested his father and removed him from the house. His mother decided that the family should go that night to stay with his grandparents. As James was packing some belongings, a police officer who had stayed behind to transport the family came into his room and asked if he was OK. James remembers feeling relieved that the officer was there, but also feeling sad and ashamed. He confided in the officer that this was a bad day to have this happen because it was his birthday. He had just turned nine. The officer paused and reached in his pocket and gave James a quarter, telling him that it was a special quarter—a lucky one that was for his birthday. James commented that he had never forgotten that simple gesture from the policeman. He kept the quarter for years, and it came to represent a turning point in his life, the moment he realized that what his father did was wrong. For James, the police officer was not only a kind person, but also represented society's condemnation of his father's violence. When James told that story, we wondered if the officer had any idea how important that simple gesture had been to James.

Even if police have only a brief encounter with a child, it can make a difference, as James's story conveys. If police do encounter children in the course of responding to a dangerous incident, we encourage them to be aware of the children, to make arrests while children are not present, to take a minute to speak reassuringly to children, to tell them that the violence isn't their fault, or to make a referral for follow-up if needed. In summary, the police may be far more important members of a child's team of caregivers than we have previously believed.

THE BASIC PRINCIPLES OF HELPING CHILDREN

This chapter has focused on what we as adults can do to help children who live with violence. As we see, there are no magic solutions or strategies. Rather, the principles of effective help for children are basic. Parents, police, and teachers play vastly different roles with children. However, they have a common capacity to respond to children. There are three critical elements in helping children cope with violence that transcend all professional disciplines. Although these principles are defined differently by parents, teachers, and police officers, the ideas behind them are the same. No matter what our role is with children, whether we are parents, teachers, police officers, or doctors, we can use these principles in our work with them.

The first and most important principle is that we must recognize the power of a nurturing, respectful, and caring relationship with an adult to help a child recover from adversity. When adults are overwhelmed by the trauma that children have experienced, they may feel ineffectual and helpless, and they forget about this basic truth. We hear this helplessness in their questions: "What is the newest treatment technique for working with these children?" or "How can I get a child to tell me everything that happened?" or "Tell me what to say to a child when she tells me about what she saw." In the face of overwhelming need, they ask for a recipe that will work for them; they want a map to show the way to help these children. The desire to find a particular helpful strategy or intervention sometimes leads professionals to forget that the basic tool of establishing relationships is the greatest weapon against hopelessness and vulnerability in children. It's not just the latest approach or a new therapeutic strategy that helps. It is the adult behind the strategy who says, "I will listen to you" or "I believe you can succeed." This finding has been borne out in the many studies done on resilience in children. A caring adult who believes in the ability of a child to succeed is a powerful antidote for adversity.

A second principle of effective intervention is to give children permission to talk, to tell their stories about what they have seen. This principle may seem self-evident. However, there are many ways that we as adults discourage children from talking. We may believe it better for children to avoid talking about painful memories or events. Particularly for young children, it is easy to hope that if they do not talk about it, they will forget. Sometimes, we don't want them to talk because their memories are too painful for us to hear, or they remind us that we, as adults, have failed to protect them. And yet the very act of sharing frightening memories with adults can be helpful, as we saw in the story of Lisa in the last chapter.

One of the first families we saw taught us about the ways in which well-meaning adults may thwart children from talking about painful feelings. A three-year-old boy named Jacob was brought to our program by his grandmother. Jacob's mother (who was this grandmother's daughter) had been murdered in her home by an unknown assailant. The grandmother had assumed guardianship of the child. We first saw them about two weeks after the mother's death at the suggestion of Jacob's pediatrician. In the first session, we saw the grandmother and child together. As the grandmother began to tell the story about what had happened, she dropped her voice to a whisper. She would not look at Jacob and refused to say the word "dead" out loud, instead spelling it in a soft whisper. Jacob sat quietly, pulling a toy or two from the shelf but not playing with them. At first he looked puzzled and then forlorn. The grandmother made no eye contact with him and almost seemed to be ignoring him. He listened to his grandmother and started to ask for "Mama." His grandmother froze and made no response to the boy. Jacob tried to engage her with a question about his mama. With no response from her, he gave up and turned away. This interaction was striking largely because of the nonverbal communication between Jacob and his grandmother. We wished that Jacob could have climbed onto his grandmother's lap and been held by her. We weren't as concerned about what words were used as we were about the emotional gulf between them. We saw two people, each paralyzed by grief, who could not use each other for comfort. What we understood (which the grandmother later confirmed) was that Jacob was not given permission to talk about his mother. In his experience, she had simply disappeared. No one talked about her and now he could not talk about her—an incomprehensible sequence of events for a three-year-old. The grandmother later explained to us that she had thought it best for Jacob if they avoided discussion about his mother. She put all pictures of her daughter away, ostensibly so that the reminders would not upset him. She confessed that she did not know how to answer Jacob's questions or how to talk to him about death. We also realized that her avoidance of this subject with her grandson had to do with the intense grief that she was experiencing. Her well-meaning effort to protect her grandson was designed to enable her to avoid her own feelings. And it wasn't helping either of them.

Our first intervention was to schedule a couple of sessions with the grandmother alone so that we could begin to acknowledge with her the enormity of her loss. We also wanted to help her decide how to talk with Jacob. We stressed that we thought it was very important to allow Jacob to talk about his mother, even though it was so hard for her to bear his questions. We talked about what language to use and recommended a book for her to read. We told her about what we had observed in the first session and emphasized that the words weren't as important as her ability to comfort Jacob and reassure him that she was there to take care of him. Within a month or so, there was a striking difference in their relationship. Even though the grief was there for both of them, they could at least bear to acknowledge it, each in his or her own way. The grandmother learned how to talk with Jacob, and thus felt much freer to respond with empathy, support, and reassurance.

A third principle of effective intervention is that we must do whatever we can, in small and large ways, to provide a safe environment for children who have witnessed violence. Obviously, we cannot always create safe neighborhoods or homes for children. Sometimes, it may seem futile to try to help if a child continues to live in a dangerous environment with little chance of being able to leave. However, there are small ways in which we can give children refuge and protection, even if we cannot address the larger environmental dangers. Helping a child figure out whom he or she can talk to when scared, or assisting a parent in creating a predictable daily routine for a child, can be enormously effective in helping that child feel more safe and secure.

CHAPTER 5

Community Responses to Children Who Witness Violence

The previous chapters focused on the impact of exposure to violence on young children and their families and described what individuals—both parents and professionals—can do to help. This chapter looks at the broader environments. What can communities do to help children? What is the role of government in identifying and intervening with children who are affected by violence? What policies or laws facilitate or hinder families' abilities to obtain help? What innovative programs are working in this area? And finally, what broader changes in our society are needed to protect children and prevent violence?

NO GOOD DEED GOES UNPUNISHED: LESSONS LEARNED FROM FLAWED POLICY INITIATIVES

When we speak to professionals about children who witness violence, we expect certain responses. The first response, mentioned earlier, is helplessness and horror. People are upset and want to know what they can do to help children. This response is universal. We hear it from teachers, police officers, health providers, and parents. The second response that quickly follows is anger. "How can these things happen?" "Why don't people do a better job of protecting their children?" We hear these responses particularly when discussing children who witness domestic violence. The anger quickly becomes focused on the parents, particularly the mother. "Why does she stay?" or "How can she let that go on in front of the children?" It is ironic to us that mothers seem to get more blame than fathers, particularly if the violence is chronic. We wonder why more people don't say, "How could he do that in front of the children?" or "Why hasn't he been arrested and thrown in jail?" At any rate, participants clearly feel anger and a need to do something to make the situation better for children. Unfortunately, this new-found zeal sometimes leads to actions that only make things worse for families.

One example of this kind of response is in the policy decisions by some states to enact additional legal penalties if an act of violence is committed in front of a child. In the state of Utah, a person can be charged with a felony for committing an act of domestic violence in front of a child. At first glance, this may appear to be a good law that might deter adults from assaulting one another in front of a child. However, this law may also lead to felony charges for both the perpetrator of the violence and the victim if she attempts to fight back. Instead of one parent being arrested and charged, two parents now may be charged. It may also result in children being required to testify against a parent, an experience that can be traumatic for a child. One could legitimately question how this law could help children since it may rob them of both parents and lead to inappropriately involving them in court proceedings. It is also worth noting that the deterrence effect of this law has not been demonstrated.

Another questionable policy that some states are adopting is to define child exposure to domestic violence as a form of child neglect. A recent article in the *New York Times* focused on a 1998 state court decision that declared incidents of domestic violence committed in the presence of children to be sufficient grounds for a woman to be charged with neglect.[1] Because every state has statutes that define child abuse and neglect and requirements that such cases be reported to the state children's protective services, the implications of defining exposure as neglect are significant. All professionals who are mandated by law to report suspected cases of child abuse or neglect would be required to report cases of domestic violence in which a child was involved. There is a certain logic to this policy. Exposure to domestic violence is harmful to children. If parents fail to protect their children from this risk, isn't this a form of child neglect? Shouldn't there be some kind of intervention to protect the child? While there is general agreement that some kind of intervention is important, the disagreement comes over what type of intervention is actually supportive. Mandatory investigations by children's protective services may not be helpful, and in some cases may actually make the situation at home worse. In addition, the nonabusing parent (usually the mother) is made to feel responsible for behavior that she had little or no control over, and indeed is blamed for not adequately protecting her child from exposure to the abuse. The story of Virginia and Sarah shows why this policy is flawed and dangerous.

Virginia, a twenty-year-old mother, brought her four-year-old daughter, Sarah, to the emergency department of a local hospital because the child was running a high fever and vomiting. Virginia mentioned to the physician that she had no money for medication. The physician, after seeing the girl, asked the hospital social worker to help Virginia obtain assistance to pay for the medication. In the course of the interview, Sarah noticed a brochure in the waiting room that gave information about resources for battered women. There was a picture on the front of a man and a woman fighting. The little girl looked at it for a minute and casually told the social worker that her dad hit her mom "just like that picture." The social worker turned to the mother, who confirmed that she had recently had an argument with her husband that resulted in him striking her, and that Sarah had been in the room at the time. In this brief interaction, the social worker gave the mother information about counseling, support groups, and shelters for battered women, and informed the mother that she would notify children's protective services of her concern that Sarah had witnessed domestic violence. The social worker filed a report with the local protective services office, which sent a worker to the home to assess the situation. The worker had very little information other than the brief report of marital violence.

The worker arrived at the home and was greeted by Virginia's husband, who knew nothing about the report. When the worker identified herself, he became furious. She did not divulge any information about the source of the complaint, but he figured out what had happened. He refused to let the worker in the house and vowed to get even with whomever had accused him of abuse. The worker left, fearful for her safety and that of the mother and child. She contacted Virginia at her job to tell her about her encounter. Virginia picked up Sarah at school and went to a family member's house instead of going home. The children's protective services opened the case for a full investigation.

In this case, an offhand remark by a young child triggered a series of events that ultimately robbed Virginia of any choice or control about her relationship with her husband. As she later said, she had thought about leaving him, but she could not afford to live on her own and she was worried that he would become more violent and unpredictable. There is no doubt that Virginia and Sarah could benefit from support and assistance. But is a report to children's protective services the best way for the family to get help? The hospital social worker had good intentions, but inadvertently made the situation more dangerous for Virginia and Sarah. She did not think about the ramifications of her report, nor did she tell Virginia in advance so that she could decide on a strategy to keep safe. For example, if the hospital social worker, the protective services worker, and Virginia had talked with one another, Virginia might have made arrangements to leave the home before the worker came out to interview the father. Virginia later said that she was astounded that she had brought her child for a medical assessment and ended up being accused of neglecting her child and having to leave home.

This case presents dilemmas that practitioners face repeatedly. How can Sarah be protected? How can Virginia be supported so that she is not made to feel blamed for the situation and guilty about her failure as a parent? How can this father be held accountable for his behavior? If we at the Child Witness to Violence Project could rewrite this scenario, we would advocate a different strategy of intervention for this family. The social worker at the hospital should have asked for more information from Virginia and her daughter about the family violence. How often did it happen? What were the worst instances? What did Sarah see or hear? Was she ever abused? Was this an isolated event or was there a pattern of behaviors? Obtaining this information would have enabled the social worker to make a more careful decision about next steps to take. Perhaps she would have learned that Virginia lived next door to her mother and that when fights began in their home, Sarah had been taught to go to her grandmother's house. Sarah knew that her parents argued and fought, but she rarely saw it happen and she was not in danger of being hurt.

States have widely differing policies about the mandated reporting of exposure to domestic violence to children's protective services. In a state that mandated a report, the social worker's actions would have been automatic. In a state that gives more leeway for decision making to the individual reporter, this case may not have been reported. One could argue that Sarah was not in danger and that Virginia was not failing to protect her daughter. In fact, she was doing everything she could to keep her safe. There is no doubt that Virginia and Sarah could benefit from support. However, a mandatory investigation by children's protective services may not provide the support they need. It would have been preferable to mobilize voluntary support services for this family, such as counseling or assistance with deciding what options would have been best for Virginia.

The tension between protecting children and making negative judgments about parenting is an issue for many professionals working with families affected by domestic violence. If the government moves to protect children, the assumption is that parents are failing to do so. There is a rich history of resentment and anger on the part of battered women's advocates toward children's protective services for their perceived insensitivity to battered women's needs. This tension also reflects the dichotomy between the privacy of family life and public responses to ensure the safety of children. Protecting both parents' rights and children's rights involves difficult and at times contradictory philosophies.

To try to bridge some of these contradictions, a growing number of communities are actively working to integrate the perspectives of battered women into the child protection arena. One of the most notable initiatives has been funded by the Edna McConnell Clark Foundation. Since 1995, the Clark Foundation has funded community child protection partnerships in four cities: Cedar Rapids, Iowa; Jacksonville, Florida; Louisville, Kentucky; and St. Louis, Missouri. All share the common goal of refocusing responsibility for the safety of children in the community away from centralized child protection bureaucracies and toward the communities in which families live. Each site has created a network of partnerships to develop comprehensive, neighborhood-based supports and services for abused and neglected children. In 1998, the Clark Foundation brought the four sites together with national domestic violence experts to focus on the challenges of integrating a domestic violence perspective into the work of child protection. From this meeting, the four sites began to plan specific strategies to bring together advocates for battered women and child protection workers. For example, Jacksonville, Florida, now has a fully integrated team that meets at Hubbard House, a shelter for battered women. This team includes battered women's advocates and child protection workers, and meets monthly to discuss families in their caseloads who are affected by domestic violence. They have developed joint protocols for screening for domestic violence and child abuse, and they provide consultation on domestic violence or child abuse if needed. In addition, workers are trained together and as part of their training shadow each other. A new child protection worker spends time at Hubbard House to better understand the perspective of battered women, and a battered women's advocate spends time with the child protection worker to understand the specific challenges of investigating allegations of abuse and neglect and attempting to provide safety for children. The staff of the Jacksonville Community Partnership are very enthusiastic about this collaboration. They believe that it has resulted in better and more carefully delivered services to their families.

SOCIAL CONTEXTS OF CHILDREN AND FAMILIES AFFECTED BY VIOLENCE

In this book, we focused on a number of children and families whose lives were shattered because of violent events. Their stories include those of horrific violence, such as Hoang and Lan, who witnessed the murder of their mother, or Wayne, who was a bystander to his friend's death. Mark, Sally, Eric, Anna, and Billy have lived with the more subtle and insidious violence of domestic abuse. Some of the children we discussed experienced intrusions into their homes or saw assaults on family members. What do these stories tell us about the failures of communities and systems of care to prevent violence or respond to these families' needs? Despite the differences in circumstances, stories, ages of children, and types of violence witnessed, these families have characteristics in common that suggest directions for improvement.

A defining characteristic of many families described in this book is that of isolation. For some families, the isolation is a product of culture and immigration. The family of Hoang and Lan in chapter 1 had immigrated from Cambodia. They were isolated in their neighborhood and had few friends. Carmen's family was isolated by poverty, unsafe housing, and Carmen's distrust of social services. For other families, the isolation is a product of domestic violence. The parents of Jenna and Ben in chapter 3 maintained secrecy about the violence in their relationship, and this secrecy isolated them both. For many families affected by domestic violence, connections to churches or social groups are tenuous or nonexistent. They do not belong to parent-teacher organizations or mothers' groups; they do not socialize with friends. They are alone with their trauma.

Another common characteristic of the families in this book is that the parents experience considerable stress, which affects their ability to be available to their children. In some instances the stress is directly related to being abused. Michelle, the mother of three in chapter 3, was so traumatized by her own abuse that she could not be responsive to her children's needs. Carmen's history of abuse, abandonment, and foster care affected the decisions she made for her children. In other cases, the stress is connected to living in unsafe areas, having inadequate housing, or struggling with poverty. In every case, the mother's mental health significantly affects the quality of the parent-child relationships. This may be evident in a child from early infancy. If a mother is depressed, preoccupied, afraid, or highly anxious, her ability to establish an attuned, consistent, connected relationship with her baby may be compromised. This absence sets the stage for numerous difficulties later in life.

A third theme echoed in the stories of many families is the difficulty of reaching out for help. Sometimes this difficulty has to do with the shame and stigma of talking about family matters. Ben and Jenna's mother did not want anyone to know what was happening in her home. Sometimes institutional barriers make it difficult to obtain help. Professionals often minimize the impact of violence on families and especially on children. Many of the parents we see in our program received help only after becoming involved either with the legal system (via the police or courts) or with children's protective services. The voluntary or informal social service system had not been effective in reaching out to these families.

A fourth theme is that when families live in poverty, their abilities to cope with violent environments are further compromised. Poverty is a pervasive and debilitating source of stress. If a family lives in a poor community, there is a significantly greater likelihood that the community will be unsafe. Lisa, who woke up at night to see an intruder at her window, lives in a neighborhood plagued with violence. Carlos, who had grown up in a violent neighborhood, said he would never feel safe outside. Children who live in high-risk neighborhoods are not only more likely to be exposed to violence, but they are less likely to get help. This reality was particularly evident at the time of the Columbine school shootings in 1999. Columbine, a comfortable, middle-class high school, received crisis mental health services from counselors who came from all over the country to assist students in the aftermath of that tragedy. These resources are often nonexistent, however, when there is a death in a poor urban school system.

Poor neighborhoods generally offer fewer social supports to families and fewer emotional buffers for children. Thus, the same act of violence may have vastly different consequences depending on the social context of neighborhoods. Consider the case of the Baker family. Sara, age eight, lived with her parents and younger brother, Wilson, age six, in a middle-class neighborhood. Sara's family had been in their house for many years and had seen the neighborhood change from a working-class community to a more affluent area. Sara's parents lived with significant stress. Her father was disabled from an automobile accident. Her mother had a history of acute depression and had been hospitalized on many occasions. Neither parent worked. In addition, both children had seizure disorders requiring regular medication. One night, Sara's mother was mugged when she was visiting a friend in another part of the city. This incident was traumatic for her mother, who had grown up with abusive parents, and triggered an emotional breakdown that led to hospitalization. Sara and her brother were left with their disabled father, who was barely able to care for them. Sara had several friends on the street with whom she played regularly. She told them about her mother being in the hospital. Word spread about the plight of her family, and neighbors offered to help. Within a few days, neighbors had organized a schedule ensuring that one or two adults visited Sara's house twice a day to bring meals, administer the children's medications, and make sure the children got to school in the morning. This system worked until their mother was released from the hospital.

What would have happened if Sara and Wilson had lived in another neighborhood? Imagine a neighborhood where residents are poor and transient, and where unemployment and crime rates are high. Neighbors don't talk to each other. There are two abandoned buildings on the street, and other housing is substandard. Sara's parents do not know their neighbors. Sara and her brother do not play outside or know other children on the street because it is not safe. While Sara's mother is in the hospital, the children attend school irregularly. When they go, teachers note that they are not clean and discover that they are not getting their medication regularly. The school makes a report to children's protective services, alleging neglect. The agency becomes involved with the family by sending out a worker and arranging for a homemaker. Although the family is grateful for the help, Sara's parents are deeply ashamed to have the agency involved with their family. They see it as a judgment about their failure as parents. Their shame further isolates them because they don't want anyone to know what has happened.

Thus, the crime against Sara's mother has profoundly different consequences for the family depending on what kind of neighborhood they live in. In social contexts that offer support and connection, the aftermath of the violence can be absorbed in a different way. Informal support systems can work. In neighborhoods where informal supports are less available, the same act of crime could have a much different outcome, making the family feel stigmatized and further isolated. While this example depicts low-income neighborhoods as unsupportive, we must be careful not to generalize this assumption. There are strength and compassion in poor neighborhoods just as there are isolation and anonymity in affluent neighborhoods.

A fifth theme that underlies much of the violence discussed in this book is the legacy of gender-specific violence. Our cultural history of viewing women as second-class citizens or as property underlies much domestic violence. These beliefs are deeply ingrained and they influence both family relationships and institutional responses. For the families in this book whose lives were marked with domestic violence, the operating assumption for the men was that it was within their rights to be abusive to their wives. This assumption is the basis of most of the domestic violence we have seen in the Child Witness to Violence Project. There was neither sufficient social pressure nor legal threat to deter men's abusive behavior. Men's logic can become quite distorted as they justify their behavior. Our society reinforces gender-related violence in countless ways: from promoting advertising or music with violent or misogynist themes to allowing courts or police to trivialize women's complaints.

PROGRAMS THAT SHOW PROMISE

These five themes suggest certain directions for change. Fortunately, there are emerging programs that address family stress and isolation, barriers to accessing services, and creating safer communities. The Child Witness to Violence Project has been involved with two such programs that offer innovative and promising strategies for change. While there are a growing number of other programs working toward the same goals, these are programs we know very well. The first is an example of an effort that involves small local social groups in an attempt to change attitudes and build awareness about domestic violence. The second is a federal government–sponsored initiative whose goal is to change community systems of care to better protect children.

The Safe Havens Interfaith Partnership against Domestic Violence

Anne Marie Hunter, an ordained Methodist minister who brings both personal and professional experience to this project, founded Boston Justice Ministries/Safe Havens in 1991. As she tells the story, her motivation to begin the project grew from her experience as a victim of domestic violence. Anne Marie grew up in the Southwest in a religious family that was deeply involved in church. She attended church weekly and thought of the church members as extended family. She married her college boyfriend at age twenty. A short time after the marriage, he began to abuse her. The abuse, both physical and psychological, was to last throughout the four years of their marriage. In a sermon she later preached about this time in her life, Anne Marie stated, "I never told anyone about the ways things were for me at home. I was much too ashamed, and I felt terribly, terribly guilty. Somehow the relationship problems seemed all my fault."

Throughout their marriage, Anne Marie continued to go to church regularly. However, she never mentioned the abuse to anyone. As she writes, "This didn't seem like the kind of thing you could talk to the priest about. The people at church all seemed so perfect. I assumed I was the only one this ever happened to. I was also afraid the priest wouldn't believe me." As things worsened in the relationship, Anne Marie grew more despondent and desperate. Finally, she decided to leave. She writes about this decision: "[I had] privileges and resources. . . . I was white; I was middle-class; I was able-bodied; I had a good job and a supportive family; I had an education and no children to provide for. I could leave."

Several months after she left her husband, she received a call from the minister at her church, who asked her to come in and talk to him. Assuming that he had heard about her separation and was offering support, she was grateful to talk. However, she soon discovered that her husband had contacted the minister and asked that he "counsel" Anne Marie about their marriage. The session was excruciating. The minister refused to believe the abuse, criticized her decision to "abandon" her marital vows, and berated her for not forgiving her husband. Anne Marie left the counseling session despairing at the failure of the minister to recognize or legitimize her experience as a battered woman. She also left the church, feeling betrayed and marginalized.

After a two-year absence from the church, Anne Marie returned, eventually deciding to become an ordained minister. Her experiences and determination to change the way religious communities responded to domestic violence shaped her decision to become a minister. She was determined that no woman should be treated as she had been.

At seminary, Anne Marie worked in a local battered women's shelter and heard countless stories from women who felt let down by the church. For many of these women, the church and their religious faith were essential parts of their lives. Few of them talked with their clergy. Some of those who sought assistance from the church were not supported, and their experiences were not validated. Biblical scripture was used to remind women that they should forgive, or to chastise them for their failure to honor their marriage vows. As one woman wryly commented, "My minister told me to get on my knees and pray harder. I did that. I now have calluses on my knees and he still beats me." Anne Marie realized that her experience was not unique. Many women shared her disbelief and sadness at the ways in which the church failed to respond to women who were being abused.

Anne Marie wrote her thesis on how clergy respond to domestic violence. For this project, she interviewed Protestant clergy from rural, suburban, and urban areas about their knowledge, attitudes, and experience with battered women in their congregations. Her findings were interesting. Most clergy had some knowledge of the social issue and believed that an abusive relationship was a serious problem that warranted assistance. They believed that it was likely to be a problem in their community but they drastically underestimated its prevalence. Eighty-two percent of the respondents indicated that they were either infrequently or never called on by their parishioners for advice about abusive relationships. Sixteen percent of the respondents did not believe that divorce was justifiable for a battered woman, or believed that only the most extreme violence would justify a divorce. When asked about training and knowledge of resources in their area, the majority of ministers had no formal training about domestic violence. They had some knowledge of resources in their communities but felt that the resources were inadequate.

These findings were paradoxical. On one hand, clergy believed that the problem existed in their communities. On the other hand, few of them had been approached to assist a congregant in need. And few clergy felt adequately prepared to respond. For Anne Marie, the need for training was clear. Over the next five years, she created the Safe Havens Interfaith Partnership to address this crucial need. In the first years, Anne Marie and her small staff organized a speaker's bureau and spoke at many religious events and institutions. They created a newsletter and a central directory of resources that clergy could access. However, the one-time workshops or lectures seemed inadequate. The information they presented might be memorable or interesting, but was it creating sustainable change within the churches? In the mid-1990s the staff at Safe Havens began to explore other options for working with church communities.

Ultimately, the design the staff created demanded that congregations commit time and resources to an educational program for one year. This training would involve both clergy and lay members. Safe Havens recruited faith communities to be a part of the first training. Every church or synagogue interested in participating was required to organize what they called a Safe Havens team, involving at least one clergy member and two lay people. Team members agreed to participate in quarterly training workshops on topics such as the dynamics of domestic violence, working with congregants who batter, the impact of domestic violence on children, teen dating violence, and religious issues affecting family violence. An intensive workshop would also be held for religious-school teachers and youth leaders. As part of the training, Safe Havens teams would meet with local service providers from battered women's programs, law enforcement, and children's services. The goal was for congregations to become familiar with the problem and equally comfortable accessing resources. The decision to involve both clergy and lay people reflected the belief of the staff that domestic violence is a community problem and that the solution should not lie just with community or religious leaders, but also with every member of the community.

In the first year, Safe Havens recruited eleven churches and synagogues with eighty participants. The group's diversity was astonishing: three synagogues from affluent areas around Boston, several churches with conservative Christian doctrines, and several liberal Protestant denominations. Collectively this group represented more than 11,000 urban and suburban residents.

This group met quarterly for formal training. These trainings brought a wide range of people together: urban, suburban, African-American, Latino, white. The common denominator was a belief in the power of religious communities to effect change in a person's life. Each session began with a biblical reflection. Clergy from the various communities led the reflection. Scriptures were chosen carefully, highlighting difficult or controversial texts in the Bible. For example, one text used was the Genesis story of the rape of Dinah. Another reflection examined the troubling passage in the book of Ephesians that exhorts wives to be subject to their husbands. Participants reflected on these passages, speaking from diverse traditions.

In between these formal training sessions, the Safe Havens

teams undertook a wide range of activities in their congregations: placing information in church bulletins, preaching sermons on topics related to family relationships and family violence, hosting educational programs for men's and women's groups, sponsoring workshops on teen dating violence for youth in the church. In addition, each faith group developed a strategy to respond to domestic violence in their communities, using the skills and resources of their particular community. The perplexing dilemma of having both the victim and the batterer in the same congregation was discussed.

The response was enormous. The clergy-led studies of biblical texts were highly valued. Both clergy and lay leaders consistently reported increased understanding of and comfort with the dynamics of family violence. They also reported that parishioners came forward to talk about violence in the family. Clergy felt better prepared to respond and had better knowledge of the resources in their areas. One minister gave an example. He was called in the middle of the night by one of his parishioners who had locked herself in the children's bedroom because her husband had threatened to kill her. She was terrified. The first person she called was the minister because he had recently preached a sermon on domestic violence. With the woman's assent, the minister called the police, who responded and arrested the man. He then helped arrange for counseling for the woman and her children. Because he considered it his duty as a minister, he initiated contact with the man and urged him to get help for his abusive behavior. The minister commented that without the training he "would have frozen" at receiving such a call. It is equally likely that he would not have received the call, because the woman would not have thought of her minister as someone she could reach out to with this personal crisis.

This training has been repeated each year since 1998. A wider variety of faith communities has been involved, including an Islamic congregation and a Roman Catholic church. The project is remarkable in its scope and thoughtful design. It uses one of the strongest institutions of society to raise consciousness about the destructive power of family violence. It increases awareness by its efforts to help congregations learn about the dangers of relationship violence and uses the language of the scripture to engage community members in thinking about the roots of family violence as depicted in the Bible. Finally, by training clergy and lay people to respond appropriately, it becomes a powerful way to identify women and children who are at risk of abuse. The openness with which the training is done reduces the stigma and the isolation so many women struggle with.

The Save Havens Interfaith Partnership is a strong example of an effort to address the issue of domestic violence, reaching people through the social bonds of community groups. It is also an example of a "bottom-up" approach to reducing domestic violence. The federal government's initiative, called "Children Exposed to Violence," is a top-down approach, and provides an example of what government can do to address this problem.

The Safe Start Initiative

In a large community room at Central Carolina Community College, ninety residents of Chatham County, North Carolina, gathered for an all-day meeting. The walls were made of cinder block and painted white. It was September; the temperature outside was ninety-five degrees. Eight long rows of tables faced the front, where there were several flip charts and an overhead projector. White tablecloths covered the tables. The group was diverse: A cluster of teenagers sat halfway back; a group of older African-American men sat on the other side. Some women wore suits; others were informally dressed. A few women came into the room with young children. Most people seemed to know one another. The task of this group was to create a strategy to reduce violence in the county. In particular their mission was to reduce violence in the lives of children. This was the first of three all-day meetings that would develop a plan to make Chatham County a safer place for families to live.

By urban standards, Chatham County was already a safe place to live. Rates of violent crime were low. There had been only seventeen murders in the past year. There were no gangs to speak of. There had been no school shootings. However, the residents spoke passionately about their concerns about violence. What was it they worried about? They talked about violence in the media; they spoke of child abuse and domestic violence. They knew the local hot spots: the trailer parks where Saturday-night drinking and drugging led to violence. They were concerned about the rising tensions in the eastern part of the county, where there has been a tenfold increase in the Hispanic population in the last decade.

They worried about new mothers who were isolated and poor. They knew that 12 percent of the children in the county lived in poverty. While there may not have been sensational, high-profile violence, it was clear that safety for families was a subject that everyone in the room felt passionately about.

Located in central North Carolina, Chatham County has a population of 46,000 spread over 707 square miles. It is a county of contrasts. The eastern part of the county borders Chapel Hill, home of the University of North Carolina and part of the Research Triangle, the thriving home of numerous pharmaceutical and biotechnology companies. There are multimillion dollar homes and gated communities. By contrast, in the western part of the county, a higher proportion of residents is poor and isolated. The one town of size, Siler City (population 5,000), has seen an explosive growth in its Hispanic population. In 1990, less than 1 percent of the school population of Siler City was Hispanic. By 2000, this figure had grown to 41 percent, leading some to say that Chatham and its two neighboring counties had the fastest growing Hispanic population in the country. The area's poultry processing plants provide jobs for the burgeoning Hispanic community. The influx of workers from Mexico has created deep resentment and animosity in the county. In February 2000, former Ku Klux Klansman David Duke organized a rally in Siler City to urge residents to take a stand against immigration and "the degeneracy of inner cities in this country." He exhorted residents of Siler City to "get these illegal immigrants out or you'll lose your homes, you'll lose your schools, you'll lose your way of life."[2] Although David Duke's visit was bitterly resented by many of the town's residents, it spoke to the racial tensions that accompany the demographic changes in the county.

Chatham County, along with eight other communities throughout the country, has received funds from the U.S. Department of Justice to establish integrated service systems to identify and intervene with children exposed to violence. The broad purpose of the grants is to prevent and/or reduce the impact of family and community violence on young children. To achieve this goal, the Justice Department directed applicants to improve access to and delivery of high-quality services to young children (and their families) at high risk of exposure to violence. This initiative will ultimately distribute several million dollars to each funded community.

This program, known as the Safe Start Initiative, is a bold example of how the federal government has attempted to create change at the local level. The communities selected for funding, nine out of 208 applications, are dramatically different in size, demographics, and culture. There are large urban areas, some strongly associated with high crime: Baltimore, Chicago, and San Francisco. There are midsize communities: Rochester, New York; Spokane, Washington; Bridgeport, Connecticut. In addition to Chatham County two other counties received funding: Pinellas County, Florida, and Washington County, Maine. The common ingredient of these locales was their vision and their determination to create communities that would be safe for children and families. Their plans would bring key agencies and constituents together to develop strategies to identify and support children exposed to violence. They defined exposure to violence as encompassing both direct victimization, including child abuse, and being a bystander to violence.

The vision of agencies working together for this goal sounds deceptively simple. The realities of getting large systems to agree on procedures, strategies, common definitions, and resource sharing can be nightmarish. The difficulties lie in the details of collaboration. The proposal that Chatham County submitted was more than 300 pages long and reflected a partnership agreement between numerous agencies throughout the county.

The nine funded communities received grants for more than three million dollars, spread over a period of five-and-a-half years, to create systems of communication and service delivery. The first nine months of this grant had to be devoted to a community assessment and planning process. Thus were scheduled the series of three community meetings that the Safe Start leadership in Chatham County held. At the end of this planning period, each community had to develop a detailed assessment of community needs and an implementation plan to meet the defined needs.

In Chatham County the coordinator of the Safe Start Initiative is a dynamic and intense woman named George Friday. By her description, George grew up in a poor community in North Carolina during the 1960s, a time when she saw her community becoming increasingly dependent on government funding for survival. She is open and articulate about the ways that this reliance on government intervention hurt her community. She passionately believes that communities and their members must develop self-reliance and that the power for leadership and self-determination comes from within the community. Trained as a community organizer, she brings this perspective to her work with Safe Start. It is perhaps an irony that she must balance her strong beliefs about community self-determination with a federal grant that has very specific guidelines about how its resources must be used. The government also has innumerable reporting requirements: forms, progress reports, mandatory conference calls, and in the current electronic age, constant e-mail requests and reminders. In fact, the bureaucratic requirements are so daunting that one community resident commented, "Chatham County might actually succeed with this project despite the federal government's involvement."

As George facilitates the meeting at the community college, she wants to hear from everyone. There are two questions before the group: "What would it take to make this community safe for children?" and "How can we reduce children's exposure to violence in Chatham County?" The participants divide into small working groups. The teenagers stick together. The groups are given specific tasks and will report back to the larger group. The discussions are focused and everyone is involved. One woman, an employee of the local children's protective services, talks about the frustration of going back to the same houses over and over again to see children who are neglected or abused. She is frustrated that the courts won't agree to remove the children. The public health home-visitor speaks of the isolation she sees in the first-time mothers she visits. One teenager remembers that his mother was visited by a local agency staff member when she gave birth to his younger sister. "They brought a basket of things for us. Could we do something like that for all mothers?"

Several residents speak of the need for more recreation facilities for teenagers. Someone asks, "How can recreation facilities make communities safe?" Several others chime in to say that if teenagers are constructively engaged, the opportunities for them to engage in violent behavior decrease.

The teenagers are talking about a campaign to make people more sensitive to television violence. They wonder if they could get a sports figure to endorse the campaign. Lunchtime comes. There is a bustle of activity in the back, and local women bring in a hot meal: fried chicken, mashed potatoes, rolls, gravy, and green beans. This is regional cooking at its best. No matter what the temperature is outside, everyone appreciates a hot meal in the middle of the day.

At the end of the day, the number of participants has dwindled. There are charts and scribbled newsprint on all four walls of the room. It is obvious that this group has worked hard. George and the staff gather the tablecloths and the newsprint and head back to the office. They are pleased with the turnout but note that no one from the Police Department was able to come. George wishes that more community residents, as opposed to agency professionals, had been able to come. There is much work to do.

Over the course of the next four months, the staff and various working committees of residents and community providers continue to meet to develop their plan.Chatham County has 3,428 children under the age of five. In the course of the community assessment, they learn that 556 calls were made to the sheriff's and police departments in the county. There were also 212 cases of confirmed child abuse or child neglect in the past year. They also learn that when a child appears in juvenile court, no one asks about whether there are other children at home or if there has been domestic violence. They learn that when police respond to a domestic violence call, there is no system for guaranteeing that the children who might have witnessed the abuse are mentioned in the police report or referred to a local service provider. There have been spirited discussions about the involvement of schools. If a teacher suspects that a child is witnessing domestic violence, does he or she have a right to secure information from the courts about the family? How do systems both protect a family's right to confidentiality and work cooperatively with other providers? Can information be shared in ways that do not violate a family's privacy? These questions turn out to be the most difficult issues for the planning group.

The plan that Chatham County developed for its Safe Start model reflects the character of the community and a strong commitment to use informal networks within neighborhoods to change attitudes and beliefs about violence. The plan encompasses both prevention and intervention. Broad goals are twofold: to decrease the number of children that are exposed to violence, and to create a support system that will identify children who are affected by violence, and respond promptly with services. For the first year, the group proposes to target the neighborhoods with the highest rate of violent crime and child abuse. The group will identify within the community informal leaders who will serve as role models and link families to services. The local mental health agencies and the police department will share personnel to facilitate both the identification of children at risk and the direct assistance to these children and their families. Special attention will be paid to developing systems of communication between law enforcement, the courts, the department of protective services, and mental health agencies.

The prevention plans for Chatham County are ambitious. The Safe Start planners want to create communities that provide more support for parents and children. They wish to make it easier for parents to seek help. They want to increase awareness among parents of the negative effects of media on children and to give parents information and support about child rearing. To do this, participants are thinking about a media campaign, a system of parent support and education groups, and creation of printed material. In addition, they wish to create a social context that encourages citizens to share the responsibility for raising all children in a safe and nurturing way.

The Safe Havens Interfaith Partnership and the Safe Start Initiative are completely different in scope, organization, leadership, and goals. However, they share a common broad mission: to create safer communities for children and families. One is a grassroots approach, operating with a small budget and an informal leadership group that uses consensus to make decisions; the other is a large government project, complete with bureaucracy and hierarchy. Both are headed by leaders who have a strong vision and the skills to communicate the message in a compelling manner.

As we consider the range of community responses, I would argue that both approaches are needed and that they complement each other. The risk of initiatives such as Safe Start is that people in Washington, D.C., have little ability and limited knowledge to make decisions about how a community uses money or organizes programs. The federal government creates a one-size-fits-all model and expects that communities will adapt. However, the strength of Safe Start is the power of its message and the solid commitment of resources to the goal of increased safety for children and families. In a society where money talks, this initiative has made a strong statement about government priorities. In the effort to take on the epidemic of violence in the United States, this powerful voice is needed.

The beauty of the Safe Havens Interfaith Partnership is that it is so responsive to local communities. It works with them at a basic level, building on informal networks and honoring the culture and belief systems of local people. By working in faith communities, it universalizes the message and communicates it to a broad range of people.

Finally, both initiatives show the power of committed leadership and strong vision. In fact, there are many programs similar to these and voices of strong leaders throughout the country who are raising fundamental concerns about children's safety and emotional health. The challenge lies in harnessing these voices to pressure national leaders to commit to a social agenda that will protect children and reduce violence.

CHAPTER 6

Creating a Safer World for Children: Reflections on the Challenges Ahead

In the Child Witness to Violence Project, we are frequently challenged to talk about solutions: "What can we do to prevent violence?" "How can we make sure that shootings such as the Columbine massacre never happen again?" People often want simple answers, and there are none. In fact, we can't even agree on a definition of the problem. This quandary is reminiscent of the fable about asking a group of blindfolded people to define an elephant by touching a portion of the beast. One person who touches the trunk describes it as an animal that is four feet tall and cylindrical. Another person who touches the ear describes it as soft and thin. A third person, who has touched the side of the elephant, pronounces that it is large and leathery. As the group continues to work at this task, they begin to argue heatedly because their definitions are so different. Although none of them is completely wrong, their perspectives limit their definitions.

And thus it is with the proposed solutions for violence in our society. Some argue that television violence, video games, or violent music lyrics are the root cause of much of the violence in society. Others point to the ready availability of guns and focus on more stringent gun control laws. Some focus on the disintegration of family cohesion or the erosion of moral codes as the problem.

Some point to our national history of rugged individualism, the wanton pursuit of land and power that supported the institution of slavery and the systematic slaughter of Native Americans. Others say that violent behavior is a biological or genetic problem. Although none of these perspectives is wrong, they do not completely answer the question either. The problem is enormously complex; the solutions are equally daunting.

There are no easy answers, no magic wands, no simple diagnostic test that will help us understand why a person is capable of an act of violence. But I believe that suggestions for future directions lie in the stories of this book and in the work of the many professionals I have met through my work with the Child Witness to Violence Project. These ideas are neither new nor original. They should not be controversial. Perhaps the common thread that unites them is a plea for this society to treat its children and families with more civility and dignity. Despite politicians' rhetoric about a safer society, a kinder and gentler nation, there is a stark unwillingness to invest in the kinds of support that will reduce poverty, support young children's emotional and intellectual development, and make the world a safer place for children.

SIX STEPS THAT WOULD MAKE A DIFFERENCE

Children must have steady, predictable, and loving relationships from birth. Ample scientific data supports the claim that healthy relationships are at the heart of children's well-being.[1] Parents are the first to offer these connections. These relationships are a strong buffer against the trauma of violence. Yet parents report that they spend less time with their children and feel constant stress to juggle the demands of work and parenting. One survey found that few parents were satisfied with the amount of time they spent with their children.[2] Seventy-two percent of parents indicated that they would prefer to stay home with their children rather than go to work. This wish crossed all income and ethnic divisions. Another researcher estimated that within the past twenty years, working adults have added 163 hours per year to their work lives, the equivalent of an extra month.[3] More time spent at work means less time spent with children. We also know that time spent with children in the early years of life is critically important. The security that children gain and the capacity to explore the world and to trust that adults can keep children safe are embedded in the early years of a child's development and in the context of the child's relationships with parents. Yet, this country has no policies for paid parental leave for childbirth and newborn care. We are, in fact, the only wealthy country that lacks a government policy of mandatory supports and protection for parenting leave.[4] Stressed and guilty middle-class parents of newborns are forced to return to work after a twelve-week leave which may be unpaid.

The poorest families are especially vulnerable. With the advent of President Clinton's welfare reform package (the Personal Responsibility and Work Opportunity Reconciliation Act, 1996), the burden on working parents has increased substantially. In twenty-two states, this welfare reform dictates that parents must return to work before the child is one year old. In three states, parents must return to work by the time their child is three months old. As women are forced to return to work, the demands for day care have skyrocketed, far exceeding the existing resources. In New York City, for example, within one year of the passage of the Welfare Reform Act, 47,871 children in the welfare system needed child care as a result of parents' return to work, and there were only 18,638 slots.[5]

For all parents, it has become increasingly difficult to spend sufficient time with children. If we can support parents to enable them to develop and maintain good relationships with their children, we will provide a powerful psychological inoculation against the effects of exposure to violence. These supports range from prenatal care to paid parental leave to more favorable child-related tax benefits.[6] They also include resources and information, made available in a range of languages and venues.

Children and families must have access to a network of skillful helpers to facilitate healing from the effects of exposure to violence. This access can be promoted in several ways. The first is through quality early childhood education and day care. The demand for and cost of child care has skyrocketed. A 1998 survey by the Children's Defense Fund found that in fifteen states tuition for quality child care exceeds the cost of public college tuition.[7] Many working families cannot afford this. The cost of child care is a greater burden for poor families who are returning to work as a result of the welfare reform policies. Many of these families, who may struggle with multiple stressors, cannot afford quality child care and are forced to leave children with unregulated, unlicensed family day care providers. The quality of these arrangements for children is erratic at best and substandard at worst.

Countless evaluative studies have confirmed that quality early childhood programs are especially beneficial for low-income, high-risk children, providing early identification of learning or developmental problems and better preparing them for entry into elementary schools. Yet Head Start, the federally funded child care program for low-income children, reaches less than half the eligible preschool-age children. Since we know that exposure to violence is associated with poverty, one could recommend that an important strategy of support for children who witness violence should be increased access to quality child care. As in other areas, this country lags behind many similarly wealthy nations in its willingness to provide a comprehensive national child care system.

The issue of quality in child care systems is as important as the availability of child care. National reports document the poor quality of many child care settings: overcrowding, poor facilities, and lack of appropriately trained staff.[8] The issue of staff training, compensation, and retention is one of the most serious problems in child care. Most child care staff are grossly underpaid and undervalued. This fact reflects how children are devalued in the United States. There is further evidence in the fact that the poorest children and those with serious behavior and developmental problems are often in the care of the lowest-paid and least-trained providers. In short, our most challenging children are cared for by those least prepared to do so. In addition, most child care programs do not have regular access to consultants who can help teachers with children who have behavior or emotional problems. Ironically, but predictably, the more high-risk the population is, the lower the staff salaries and the fewer supports there are in the classroom. If we can provide skilled support to children at an early age, we can make a big difference in their futures.

Another set of skilled helpers that children and families need are mental health counselors. Children who are traumatized need mental health intervention, yet many are unable to secure services. Many states report critical shortages of mental health services for children. The managed health care bureaucracy limits both access to mental health care and the treatment itself. For example, in the Child Witness to Violence Project, our model of treatment includes extensive collaborative work with other providers in a child's life, particularly the teacher or day care provider. In some cases this model may include consultation with the teacher to devise strategies for support in the classroom. In other cases, if the child is involved in court proceedings about contested custody or visitation, considerable work must be done with legal professionals to advocate for decisions that reflect the child's best interests. This collateral work done on behalf of children is a time-consuming yet critical aspect of good treatment. Few managed care insurance companies, however, reimburse providers for this work. In the insurer's world, most activities outside face-to-face therapeutic contact are unworthy of recognition.

A third set of skilled helpers is pediatricians who are knowledgeable about the impact of violence on children and who can ask important questions during pediatric visits to screen for a child's experiences with violence in the home or community. Since virtually all children interact with the pediatric health system at various times during their infancy and childhood, this setting is an important one for providing early identification of children who are vulnerable and for connecting them with services. To do this screening well, pediatric providers need training and support. It is often easy for pediatricians to ask the questions, but far more difficult to know what to do with the answers. Health providers must be sensitive to the impact on the family of discussing these matters, they must be aware of their state's policies about reporting to children's protective services, and they must have resources available for families to use.

Adults must assume the responsibility of setting standards of respect, civility, and nonviolence for children. This responsibility extends across every domain of society: the home, schools, and the community. In our therapeutic work with children, we reassure them that the violence that occurs in their lives is not their fault. We also tell them that it is not their responsibility to solve the problems of adult-initiated violence. This responsibility lies with the adults. In many ways, we adults have failed our children. We hear increasing numbers of incidents in which parents are yelling at or even assaulting coaches or referees at their children's sporting events. In Boston, a parent of a fifth-grade child was arrested recently for assaulting a teacher in the classroom. Automobile drivers become enraged over seemingly minor incidents on the roads, and respond by attacking other motorists. Adults yell at each other, use degrading language, and set poor examples for children about how to behave in appropriate and respectful ways.

Within the context of home and family, parents are the first and best teachers of children. Parents give children a moral framework to live by and show children, often by example, how to live in relationship with other people. Parents have important opportunities to teach children principles of respect and tolerance and how to resolve conflict positively. Harsh disciplinary practices, negative or critical interactions with children, or explosive anger toward children teach them the wrong lessons. Parental disputes that are characterized by loud arguing, threats, or physical assaults also give children the wrong messages. Disputes between parents are a natural part of adult relationships. However, they can be frightening for children or can represent negative ways to handle disagreement. If parents can model resolution of arguments through compromise, humor, or reasonable dialogue, they give children powerful skills for handling disagreements themselves. By providing interpretation and opinions, parents shape children's understanding of the world and their emerging sense of right and wrong.

In school and child care environments there also exist many opportunities to teach children concern for others. Schools have enormous potential to create climates of respect and tolerance. Unfortunately, students are often allowed to bully or harass each other. Teachers openly criticize students or use harsh language in their interactions with students. Some states allow corporal punishment in schools, a practice that sends the wrong message about the use of force as discipline.

At the societal level, the themes of harsh punishment, anger, and disrespect are everywhere. Radio and television talk shows are replete with guests and hosts who blame, ridicule, and criticize. There is an increasing trend in the juvenile justice system to lock up younger offenders and/or to try them as adults. The most striking example of this trend is the recent decision of a Florida judge to sentence a fourteen-year-old boy to life imprisonment for the murder of an eight-year-old, a crime that was committed when the boy was twelve. While there is no denying that the crime was horrendous, what does it say about a country that treats its young teenagers in the same way it treats adults, by removing all possibilities of rehabilitation or restoration? One could argue that this action is a form of state-sanctioned violence and is immoral. The same argument has been made against the death penalty in this country, which may be handed down erroneously or applied in a prejudicial manner. Our criminal justice policies are often harsh and discriminatory, and contribute to a climate of punitive anger.

To reduce violence in communities and homes, we must reduce poverty in the United States. All families should have a basic right to be able to raise their children in safe environments. In many poor neighborhoods, this right is not assured. Poverty and violence are inextricably linked or, as Gandhi said, "Poverty is the worst form of violence." It is well established that rates of violent crime are highest in the communities with fewest resources. When police departments map violent crime in their cities, the clusters inevitably fall in the neighborhoods with the lowest family incomes, highest rates of unemployment, and poorest housing. These areas also typically have higher rates of infant mortality, reported child abuse, and chronic illness in children. Although domestic violence occurs in all communities and across all income levels, the rates of domestic violence in communities vary with income. In their 1990 National Family Violence Survey, Richard Gelles and Murray Straus found that rates of "abusive violence" against women with annual incomes below $10,000 were more than 3.5 times those found in households with incomes of $40,000 and above.[9] It stands to reason that the stressors of poverty and the concomitant lack of supports in the community lead to increased aggression and violence within the family.

In a country with the wealth of the United States, it is inexcusable that families continue to live in poverty. The latest government estimates are that more than twelve million children, or roughly one in six, live in poverty.[10] Despite twenty years of an increasingly strong economy, child poverty increased by 15 percent between 1979 and 1998.[11] This rate is the highest of any wealthy nation, compared with 9 percent in Canada, 4 percent in Germany, and 2 percent in Japan. It is also worth noting that the income level that defines official poverty in this country is shockingly low: just under $14,000 for a family of three. It is almost inconceivable to imagine how a family could live on this amount of money, particularly in urban areas where rents and costs of transportation and services are so high. If fact, nearly 40 percent of U.S. children live in families with incomes under $22,000.

The quantity and quality of poverty in this country are a moral disgrace. This poverty has particularly devastating consequences for very young children. Children lack safe housing, adequate medical care, and in some cases adequate nutrition. Single mothers account for the large majority of homeless families (70 to 90 percent depending on the study); one in four homeless persons was a child under eighteen.[12] Nearly eleven million children are without health insurance, two-thirds without coverage for six or more months. More than 13 million children under the age of twelve are hungry for part of each month.[13] For families who live with this kind of poverty, the stresses of violence are more difficult to withstand. The cumulative effects rob many parents of their emotional capacities to support their children.

We must tackle the problem of poverty by returning it to the top of a national agenda. In this time of growing economic prosperity for so many, poverty has become more invisible. During the first of several presidential debates between Al Gore and George Bush, poverty was not even mentioned. Public safety, crime, and gun violence are issues on the national horizon—not poverty, despite the undeniable connection between violence and poverty.

We must create a social climate that makes violence against women and children unacceptable. Crime statistics tell the story about male violence against women. Thirty percent of all female murder victims were killed by an intimate partner, as compared to two percent of males.[14] Of the one million violent crimes committed by intimate partners or former girlfriends or boyfriends, 85 percent of the victims are women.[15] Women and girls are victims of sexual assault with much higher frequency than males. Despite the many advances that women have made in the forty years since the feminist revolution of the 1960s, women are still discriminated against. The lyrics of popular music are peppered with references to violence against women. MTV videos beam these images to millions of households. At a basic level, we must ask ourselves why a man would assume that it is acceptable to assault or threaten a woman. We must work to create a social climate in which such violence is intolerable.

The child abuse statistics are also sobering, particularly for children under the age of six. In fact, infants represent almost 40 percent of reported victims of child maltreatment. Nationally, an estimated 2.8 million children were reported as suspected child abuse or neglect cases in 1998.[16] These numbers would be reduced if we increased social and professional supports to all new parents, provided ongoing parenting education about children and child development to all families, and developed better strategies to identify and support high-risk families.

Each of us can be an advocate for children's safety and well-being. We know that parents are very concerned about violence in the lives of their children. In a 1999 national survey conducted by *Parents* magazine, parents ranked violence as a top worry.[17] Seventy-five percent of parents surveyed worried about violence in the schools. Thirty-three percent worried about violence and danger outside the home. One in five parents knew a child who had been a victim of violence. Forty-three percent of parents with children between the ages of six and twelve said that they knew a child who was capable of violence. Families with lower incomes worried somewhat more, as did African-American and Hispanic families. However, more than one-half of higher-income families "worried a great deal" and more than 90 percent of these families "worried somewhat" about violence-related issues.

This survey reminds us that it is not just poor or inner-city parents who worry about safety. This concern appears to be an equal-opportunity preoccupation. The pervasive worries of parents should be a catalyst for change. And this concern isn't limited to parents. Young people, single people, and older citizens share the worry about violence in this country. What would it take to begin to create a safer world for children? What if we could harness this concern to affect legislation and policy in this country? We must use the power of our concern and knowledge at the ballot box. We should vote for political candidates who pledge to pursue a strong children's agenda.[18] The Children's Defense Fund, a leading national advocacy group for children, proposes several legislative priorities: increasing the minimum wage nationally, health insurance for all children, and subsidized housing for homeless and inadequately housed children. To that list, we might add changes in the tax law to give more support to families—both an increase in the earned income tax credits and an increase in the exemption allowed for children. Another priority that is more specifically focused on violence prevention is increased regulation of gun sales and ownership. If we can create a groundswell of support for an agenda that supports families and children, we take a small step toward creating a safer society. We can write letters; we can be vocal in our schools and places of worship. In short, we have the power of our concern for children, our experiences, our purchasing power, and our votes to effect change. We should not hesitate to use them.

Noted psychiatrist and author Judith Herman writes: "When traumatic events are of human design, those who bear witness are caught in the conflict between victim and perpetrator. It is morally impossible to remain neutral in this conflict. The bystander is forced to take sides."[19] In a sense, we are all bystanders to the violence that children witness. If we remain passive bystanders to the violence, we have made a moral choice that is not tenable. We must take the side that decries the violence and demands its end. To do less is to fail in our basic responsibilities to all children in our society.

APPENDIX

Talking with Young Children about Terrorism and War

Betsy McAlister Groves, Judy Hunt, and Maxine Weinreb

The events of September 11, 2001, were overwhelming and incomprehensible for all. Parents faced the task of deciding what to tell their children and how to tell them in a way that provided the necessary information but was not too scary for them. This was not easy because we as adults did not have all the answers, and many of us were frightened and worried about this terrible disaster and its aftermath.

We at Boston Medical Center's Child Witness to Violence Project received many questions about the best ways to talk to children about the events, and we put together the following information in order to give parents such guidance. These guidelines are focused on children eight and younger, although many of the principles apply to older children. They come from our experience working with young children who witness community and domestic violence and from our understanding of child development. In our work, we have learned a great deal about how young children think about violence and how adults can help them cope with the fears and anxieties that often come as a result of exposure to traumatic violence.

Before you talk to your child, it is important that you take stock of your own thoughts, beliefs, and reactions. Children, especially young children, are keenly aware of their parents' emotional responses. Your feelings and responses give children important cues about how they should react. If parents communicate a great deal of worry or fear, their children may react similarly. Events like those of September 11 and thereafter present opportunities to teach children lessons about death, war, hatred, and racism, all difficult but important topics to discuss with children. Because we as adults are likely to have strong feelings about these events, it is also important that we have support and connection with others so that we are not alone with these intense feelings.

Your relationship with your child as a parent or caregiver is the most important ingredient of help that you provide. Your ability to hear your child's worries, to accept them, and to provide comfort is the foundation of any discussion about a scary event. If you as a parent or caregiver are able to keep the communication open and be available for your child, you have laid the foundation for providing the best support possible.

It is important to remember that young children communicate their thoughts and worries in more ways than by verbal expression alone. Children may draw pictures or use dramatic play or storytelling to tell us their thoughts. We can help by making sure that children are given multiple ways to communicate and that we are sensitive to reading cues from these different expressions.

All families are different. Families cope with stress in many ways, using strengths that are drawn from religious or spiritual beliefs, traditions, and relationships. There is no set script of words to use. The information we provide here is intended to give parents some guidelines to think about. It is not comprehensive, nor does it take into account every situation a parent may face. We hope it is helpful to support parents and caregivers as we face the future.

Common Questions from Parents

Should I talk about terrorism with my child? Perhaps because he/she is so young, I should not mention it.
It is almost inevitable that your child will have heard something about the September 11 terrorist attacks, the U.S. military actions

in the war on terrorism, or further terrorist threats. Even a three-year-old may hear words or observe adults who are upset or worried. It is far better that your child get information about what happened from you than from another source. By initiating a discussion about it, you give the message that it is OK to ask questions and to talk about it again.

How do young children understand terrible events such as those of a major terrorist attack?

Children's capacity to understand depends on age and ability to comprehend the world. They will not understand events in the same ways that adults do. They may know about an event because they hear adults talking or see the news, but they cannot really understand the complexities of these events. In the absence of information that is geared to their age level, they may make up their own version of the story. Here is a general summary of how children may think about events like those of September 11:

Toddlers: They will have no understanding of the events apart from the reactions of their parents or caregivers. They are sensitive to the emotions and stress level of their parents. The ways that parents manage feelings of anger, sadness, or worry affect a child's reaction.

Pre-schoolers: They have more ability to understand and, if curious or concerned, are deserving of a brief explanation. However, they may question whether these events are real or not. Their capacities for distinguishing reality from fantasy are limited. Their main worry is likely to be about the safety of their parents and themselves: "Who will take care of me?"

Kindergarteners: They will have more understanding of cause and effect, but they still see the world in reference to themselves. For example, one five-year-old's first response when she heard the news of the September 11 attacks was to ask if she would be safe the next week when her family traveled to Disney World. Children will worry about safety, about whether the perpetrators have been arrested. They may be afraid to get on an airplane or be in a tall building.

Young school-age children: They have a sense of right and wrong, good and evil, and will be more focused on why this happened. They think in absolute terms; there is no gray area as children of this age attempt to make sense out of these events. They will need more information. They, too, may voice worries about their families and fears about airplanes or tall buildings.

How or what should I tell my child?

Deciding what to tell your child is difficult. It is very important to start by asking if the child has heard anything about what happened. This gives you an opportunity to learn what the child knows, how he or she knows it, and what misunderstandings your child may have about the events. Children should have access to the basic information, but only as much information as they can understand. The decision about how much to tell a child depends on the child's age and developmental stage. A three-year-old needs different information than does a six-year-old. For example, to a three- or four-year-old who is curious or concerned about the events of September 11, you might say: "This is hard to talk about. I want to tell you about a bad thing that happened. An airplane hit some big buildings. Lots of people were hurt and some people died. Many people are sad about this. But we are safe and I will take good care of you." To questions or worries about war, you might say, "Soldiers are fighting in another country. It is far away from here. You are safe."

For a five- or six-year-old, the explanation would be somewhat different. "This is hard to talk about. A lot of people are talking about a bad thing that happened. An airplane that was flying in the air hit some big buildings. It happened in New York and Washington. Lots of people were hurt and some people died. The police and rescue workers are helping to take care of the people. We are sad about this." Or " Soldiers from our country are fighting in Afghanistan, a country that is far away. They are fighting so that we will be safe in this country."

For a seven- or eight-year-old: " You may have heard about an awful thing that has happened. Some people stole airplanes and made them fly into some big buildings in New York and Washington. Many people were hurt and some died. These people were angry and what they did was wrong. We don't know exactly why they did it. This has never happened before and we hope it won't happen ever again." Or "The President of the United States has sent soldiers to another country, Afghanistan, to try to find the people who did this, so that it won't happen again."

All children need reassurance that we as parents are doing everything we can to keep them safe. Any discussion about violent incidents should include reassurances about the child's safety and the safety of the parent/family. In addition, you may wish to add that the leaders of our country and many policemen and other helpers are working to make sure that this does not happen again. Depending on your views of the appropriateness or morality of the war, you may add that you hope the war does not last long, or that we find better ways to keep this country safe.

How should I expect my child to react to this kind of information?
Children will react in a range of ways. The reaction depends on the age, personality, and developmental ability of the child to understand the complexities of the events. Some will ask many questions. Others may show little reaction. Some common reactions may include: more worries about safety, asking the same questions repeatedly, asking no questions and not wanting to talk about it, sleep problems or bad dreams, increased clinginess with parents or caregivers, increased preoccupation with the tragedy or daydreaming, or reverting to less mature behaviors (thumbsucking, for example). These reactions are normal reactions to abnormal events, and parents should not worry about them. It takes time for all of us to calm down from events like these.

Some children will be preoccupied with worry or questions about terrorists or violent conflict. "Why did they do it?" "Will they be caught?" "Will they go to jail (or be punished)?" "Will there be a war here?" This preoccupation is normal because young children are in the process of developing morals and an understanding of right, wrong, and consequences for behavior. In addition, these questions can reflect the basic fears of safety. The underlying question is "Am I safe?" or "Is my family safe?"

Some children will have no apparent reaction and seem unconcerned or glib about what they are told. Others may laugh or make an inappropriate response to the news. They may seem to be callous or uncaring about the gravity of the situation. Children have different ways of taking in information and parents should not worry about these reactions. Parents should not push a child to talk about it but rather leave the possibility open for future discussion.

When should I worry about my child's reactions to traumatic news?
Remember that children's responses to terrible catastrophe are usually appropriate and understandable. Some children will be preoccupied for a few days; others may continue to talk about it for several weeks. In the longer-term aftermath of events like the September 11 attacks, we can expect that children (and adults) will continue to be worried, anxious, irritable, and uncertain. Some children may not talk about it for days or weeks or longer. If the intensity of your child's reaction does not diminish or if your family has been more directly affected by the tragedy, you may consider outside help for your child. If your family has suffered other stresses or losses, your child's reactions may be more intense. If your child's reactions are noticeably different from those of his/her peers, you may want to seek advice. Remember that you know your child better than anyone, and if you are worried, seek help. You may talk with other parents, your child's teacher, the school psychologist or guidance counselor, or your child's pediatrician to get advice on how to help your child. Even very young children may benefit from therapeutic intervention if they are extremely distressed.

Summary: Do's and Don'ts for Parents

- Take the time to be aware of your own feelings and reactions. Children are keenly aware of their parent's emotions and worries. If you are too upset, anxious, or worried about troubling current events, wait to talk with your child, or ask someone else who is close to them to do so.
- Be willing to talk to your child about terrorist attacks and military actions.
- Limit your child's access to television, newspapers, and magazines with graphic images of violence. For very young children, avoid exposure to the media altogether.
- Spend extra time with your children if possible. Be available to answer questions.
- Offer children various ways to communicate their worries. For some children, drawing a picture or using puppets or dramatic play is a way to express worry or to work out answers to questions.
- Take your child's questions seriously and be prepared to answer the same question repeatedly.
- Give your child enough information to answer his or her questions, but no more.
- Don't worry if your child does not talk about these subjects very much. Children have different styles and timetables for processing information.
- Pay attention to bedtime routines and take extra time for being close to your child.
- Maintain the daily routine. Predictability and routine are comforting for children.
- Offer your child opportunities to help or to do something positive. Children feel better when they can offer concrete assistance.

NOTES

1. Violence in the Lives of Young Children

1 J. Osofsky et al., "Chronic Community Violence: What Is Happening to Our Children?" *Psychiatry* 56 (1993): 36–45.

2 R. Pynoos, and S. Eth, "Children Traumatized by Witnessing Acts of Personal Violence: Homicide, Rape, or Suicide Behavior," in *Post-Traumatic Stress Disorder in Children* (Washington D. C.: American Psychiatric Press, 1985), 19–43.

3 L. Taylor et al., "Exposure to Violence among Inner City Parents and Young Children," *Developmental and Behavioral Pediatrics* 15, no. 1 (1994): 20–123.

4 Several papers were published as a result of our early work: B. Groves et al., "Silent Victims: Children Who Witness Violence," *Journal of the American Medical Association* 269, no. 2 (1993): 262–64; B. Groves, "Growing up in a Violent World: The Impact of Family and Community Violence on Young Children and Their Families," *Topics in Early Childhood Special Education* 17, no. 1 (1997): 74–102; M. Augustyn et al., "The Impact of Children's Exposure to Violence," *Contemporary Pediatrics* 12, no 8 (1995): 35–57; B. Zuckerman et al., "Silent Victims Revisited: Children Who Witness Domestic Violence," *Pediatrics* 96, no. 3 (1995): 511–13; B. Groves, "The Effects of Witnessing Violence on Very Young Children," *Harvard Mental Health Letter* 11, no. 7 (1994): 8.

5 D. Weber, "First Hub Homicide a Mother of Three," *Boston Herald,* 9 January 1992.

6 J. Twitchell, *Preposterous Violence: Fables of Aggression in Modern Culture* (New York: Oxford University Press, 1989).

7 E. O. Wilson, and S. Landry, *Sociobiology: The Abridged Edition* (Cambridge, Mass.: Harvard University Press, 1980).

8 Statistics from the Children's Defense Fund Web site: http://www.childrensdefensefund.org/gunsfacts.htm.

9 J. Meyrowitz, *No Sense of Place: The Impact of Electronic Media on Social Behavior* (New York: Oxford University Press, 1985).

10 G. Comstock, and V. Strasburger, "Deceptive Appearances: Television Violence and Aggressive Behavior," *Journal of Adolescent Health Care* 11, no. 1 (1990): 31–44.

11 Center for Media and Public Affairs Web site: http://www.cmpa.com/archive/viol/95.htm.

12 V. C. Strasburger, and E. Donnerstein, "Children, Adolescents, and the Media: Issues and Solutions," *Pediatrics* 103, no. 1 (1999): 129–39.

13 A. Bandura, D. Ross, and S. A. Ross, "Imitation of Film-Mediated Aggressive Models," *Journal of Abnormal Social Psychology* 66 (1963): 3–11.

14 T. B. Williams, ed., *The Impact of Television: A Natural Experiment in Three Communities* (New York: Academic Press, 1986).

15 R. S. Drabman, and M. H. Thomas, "Does Media Violence Increase Children's Tolerance for Real-Life Aggression?" *Developmental Psychoiogy* 10 (1974): 418–21.

16 D. Grossman, and G. DeGaetano, *Stop Teaching Our Kids to Kill* (New York: Crown Publishers, 1999), 65–81.

17 D. Caruso, "Digital Commerce," *New York Times*, 26 April 1999.

18 M. Griffiths, "Violent Video Games and Aggression: A Review of the Literature," *Aggression and Violent Behavior* 4, no. 2 (1999): 201–12.

19 J. Edelson, "Children's Witnessing of Adult Domestic Violence," *Journal of Interpersonal Violence* 14, no. 8 (1999): 839–70.

20 L. Walker, *The Battered Women's Syndrome* (New York: Springer-Verlag, 1984).

21 R. Cohen, and L. Smolan, *A Day in the Life of America* (New York: Collins Publishers, 1986).

2. The Effects of Exposure to Violence on Young Children

1 R. Watson, "It's a Scary World," *Newsweek*, 1 May 1995, 53.

2 See L. Terr, "Psychic Trauma in Children: Observations following the Chowchilla School-Bus Kidnapping," *American Journal of Psychiatry* 138, no. 1 (1981): 14–19; "Chowchilla Revisited: The Effects of Psychic Trauma Four Years after a School-Bus Kidnapping," *American Journal of Psychiatry* 140 (1983): 1543–50; *Too Scared to Cry* (New York: Harper and Row, 1990).

3 American Psychiatric Association, *Diagnostic and Statistical Manual of Mental Disorders,* 3d ed. (Washington, D.C.: American Psychiatric Association, 1980).

4 B. Perry, "Incubated in Terror: Neurodevelopmental Factors in the 'Cycle of Violence,'" in *Children in a Violent Society,* ed. J. Osofsky (New York: Guilford Press, 1997).

5 C. H. Zeanah, and M. S. Scheeringa, "The Experience and Effects of Violence in Infancy," in Osofsky, *Children in a Violent Society.*

6 S. Wieder, ed., *Diagnostic Classification of Mental Health and Developmental Disorders of Infancy and Early Childhood* (Arlington, Va.: Zero to Three/National Center for Clinical Infant Programs, 1994).

7 L. Terr, "Children's Memories in the Wake of *Challenger,*" *American Journal of Psychiatry* 153, no. 5 (1996): 618–25.

8 L. Terr, "What Happens to Early Memories of Trauma? A Study of Twenty Children under the Age of Five at the Time of Documented Traumatic Events," *Journal of the American Academy of Child and Adolescent Psychiatry* 27, no. 1 (1988): 96–104.

9 Terr, 1996.

10 Ibid.

11 M. Sugar, "Toddlers' Traumatic Memories," *Infant Mental Health Journal* 13, no. 3 (1992): 245–51.

12 S. Toth, and D. Cicchetti, "Remembering, Forgetting, and the Effects of Trauma on Memory: A Developmental Psychopathology Perspective," *Development and Psychopathology* 10 (1998): 589–605.

13 See S. Ceci, and M. L. Huffman, "How Suggestible Are Preschool Children? Cognitive and Social Factors," *Journal of the American Academy of Child and Adolescent Psychiatry* 36, no. 7 (1997): 948–58; G. S. Goodman et al., "Predictors of Accurate and Inaccurate Memories of Traumatic Events Experienced in Childhood," *Consciousness and Cognition* 3 (1994): 269–95.

14 For a helpful synthesis of Piaget's theories of development, see D. G. Singer, and T. A. Revenson, *A Piaget Primer: How a Child Thinks* (New York: Penguin Books, 1996).

15 R. Karr-Morse, and M. Wiley, *Ghosts from the Nursery: Tracing the Roots of Violence* (New York: The Atlantic Monthly Press, 1997).

3. When Home Isn't Safe: Children and Domestic Violence

1 C. Rennison, and S. Welchans, *Intimate Partner Violence,* Bureau of Justice Statistics Special Report (Washington, D.C.: U.S. Department of Justice, 2000).

2 L. Gordon, *Heroes of Their Own Lives: The Politics and History of Family Violence: Boston 1880–1960* (New York: Viking, 1988).

3 R. Pynoos, and S. Eth, "Children Traumatized by Witnessing Acts of Personal Violence"; J. Garbarino et al., *Children in Danger: Coping with the Consequences of Community Violence* (San Francisco: Jossey Bass, 1992); Terr, *Too Scared to Cry;* P. G. Jaffe, D. A. Wolfe, and S. K. Wilson, *Children of Battered Women* (Newbury Park, Calif.: Sage Press, 1990).

4 E. M. Cummings, and P. Davies, *Children and Marital Conflict: The Impact of Family Dispute and Resolution* (New York: Guilford Press, 1994).

5 E. M. Cummings, R. J. Iannotti, and C. Zahn-Wexler, "The Influence of Conflict between Adults on the Emotions and Aggression of Young Children," *Developmental Psychology* 21 (1985): 495–507.

6 E. M. Cummings et al., "Children's Responses to Different Forms of Expressions of Anger between Adults," *Child Development* 60 (1989): 1392–404; "Resolution and Children's Responses to Interadult Anger," *Developmental Psychology* 27 (1991): 462–70.

7 J. L. Edleson, "Children's Witnessing of Adult Domestic Violence," *Journal of Interpersonal Violence* 14, no. 8 (1999): 839–70.

8 C. H. Zeanah, "Assessment and Treatment of Infants Exposed to Violence," in *Hurt, Healing, and Hope,* ed. J. Osofsky and E. Fenechel (Arlington, Va.: Zero to Three, 1994), 29–37; M. Drell, C. Siegal, and T. Gainsbauer, "Post-Traumatic Stress Disorder," in *Handbook of Infant Mental Health,* ed. C. H. Zeanah (New York: Guilford Press, 1993), 291–304.

9 R. Famularo, T. Fenton, and R. Kinscherff, "Child Maltreatment and the Development of Post-Traumatic Stress Disorder," *American Journal of Diseases of Children* 147 (1993): 755–59.

4. What We Can Do to Help Children Who Have Witnessed Violence

1 A. Freud, and J. Burlingham, *War and Childhood* (New York: Medical War Books, Ernest Willard, 1943).

2 C. Dickstein, "Broken Mother, Shattered Child," *Boston Globe,* 3 February 1995.

3 Steven, Parker, M.D., personal communication, 2001.

5. Community Responses to Children Who Witness Violence

1 S. Sengupta, "Tough Justice: Taking a Child When One Parent Is Battered," *New York Times*, 8 July 2000.

2 N. Glascock, "Rally Divides Siler City," *Raleigh News and Observer*, 20 February 2000.

6. Creating a Safer World for Children: Reflections on the Challenges Ahead

1 National Research Council and Institute of Medicine, *From Neurons to Neighborhoods: The Science of Early Childhood Development* (Washington, D.C.: National Academy Press, 2000).

2 Penn, Schoen and Berland Associates, and Luntz Research, *A View of Contemporary Parenthood at the Beginning of the Twenty-first Century*, survey sponsored by *Parents* magazine and the I Am Your Child Foundation, February 2000.

3 S. Hewlett, C. West, and E. West, *The War against Parents* (Boston: Houghton Mifflin, 1998), 71.

4 Ibid., 94.

5 V. Polakow, "Savage Policies: Systemic Violence in the Lives of Children," in *The Public Assault on America's Children* (New York: Teacher's College Press, 2001), 5.

6 For a discussion of the economics of child rearing, see Hewlett, West, and West, *The War against Parents*, 89–109.

7 Children's Defense Fund, *The State of America's Children: Yearbook* (Washington, D.C.: Children's Defense Fund, 1998).

8 Center for the Child Care Workforce Web site: www.ccw.org.

9 M. Straus, and R. Gelles, *Physical Violence in American Families* (New Brunswick, N.J.: Transaction, 1990).

10 Children's Defense Fund Web site: www.childrensdefensefund.org.

11 National Center for Child Poverty Web site: http://cpmcnet.columbia.edu/dept/nccp.

12 Polakow, "Savage Policies," 7.

13 Ibid.

14 Bureau of Justice Statistics, *Violence against Women: Estimates from the Redesigned Survey* (Washington, D.C.: U.S. Department of Justice, 1995).

15 Rennison and Welchans, *Intimate Partner Violence.*

16 Administration for Children and Families, U.S. Department of Health and Human Services, "HHS Reports New Child Abuse and Neglect Statistics," *HHS News* (Washington, D.C.: Administration for Children and Families Press Room, April 10, 2000).

17 *A View of Contemporary Parenthood.*

18 See the Resources section of this book for a list of advocacy groups that provide information about legislation affecting children.

19 J. Herman, *Trauma and Recovery* (New York: Basic Books, 1992), 7.

SELECTED RESOURCES FOR PARENTS AND PROFESSIONALS

This section provides contact information about the programs mentioned in this book and resources for additional information. The list is short and is in no way intended to be comprehensive. There are many excellent sources of information about children who are exposed to violence. This list contains educational material developed by the Child Witness to Violence Project and other resources that we have found particularly valuable in our work.

Programs Mentioned in the Book

THE CHILD WITNESS TO VIOLENCE PROJECT
Boston Medical Center, MAT 5
One Boston Medical Center Place
Boston, MA 02118
Tel.: (617) 414-4244

CHILDREN EXPOSED TO VIOLENCE INITIATIVE/
SAFE START
Project Coordinator, Kristen Kracke
Child Protection Division
Office of Juvenile Justice and Delinquency Programs
U.S. Department of Justice
810 Seventh Street, N.W.
Washington, DC 20531
Tel.: (202) 616-3649

EDNA MCCONNELL CLARK FOUNDATION
Community Partnerships for Child Protection
250 Park Avenue, Suite 900
New York, NY 10177-0026
Tel.: (212) 551-9100

SAFE HAVENS INTERFAITH PARTNERSHIPS
AGAINST DOMESTIC VIOLENCE
131 Cambridge Street
Boston, MA 02114
Tel.: (617) 227-6992

Resources for Parents

Alexander, D. W. *Children Changed by Trauma: A Healing Guide.* Oakland, Calif.: New Harbinger, 1999.

Brooks, R., and S. Goldstein. *Raising Resilient Children.* Chicago: Contemporary Books, 2001.

Cummings, M., and P. Davies. *Children and Marital Conflict: The Impact of Family Dispute and Resolution.* New York: Guilford Press, 1994.

Monahon, C. *Children and Trauma: A Parent's Guide to Helping Children Heal.* New York: Lexington Books, 1993.

www.bcm.tmc.edu/cta: The Child Trauma Academy Web site, created and maintained by Bruce Perry and colleagues at the Baylor College of Medicine and the Texas Children's Hospital. The site provides a wealth of information for parents, caregivers, and professionals about children and trauma.

Resources for Teachers

Levin, D. *Teaching Young Children in Violent Times: Building a Peaceable Classroom.* Cambridge, Mass.: Educators for Social Responsibility, 1994.

Slaby, R., et al. *Early Violence Prevention: Tools for Teachers of Young Children.* Washington, D.C.: National Association for the Education of Young Children, 1995.

The Safe Havens Training Project: Helping Teachers and Child Care Providers Support Children and Families Who Witness Violence in Their Communities, 1998. Developed by Family Communications, Inc., producers of *Mister Roger's Neighborhood,* with the Child Witness to Violence Project at Boston Medical Center. This video-based training program includes three mini-documentaries about children and violence and complete workshop materials to provide training to teachers of young children. It is available from Family Communications, Inc., 4802 Fifth Avenue, Pittsburgh, PA 15213; tel.: (412) 687-2990. For a preview of the materials look at the Web site: http://www.fci.org/early_care/violence_main.asp.

Let's Talk about Living in a Dangerous World, 1995. This violence prevention program for elementary-school-age children was designed by the Erikson Institute to be used by teachers and other professionals who work with children to begin a discussion with them about the meaning and effects of violence in their daily lives. It is available from the Family Life Development Center, Cornell University, MVR Hall, Ithaca, NY 14853; tel.: (607) 255-7794.

Resources for Police Officers

Kids and Cops: Making the Connections, 2000. A fifteen-minute training video developed by the Child Witness to Violence Project and the Boston Police Department to introduce officers to key principles of child development as they relate to policing, and to give basic information about how exposure to violence affects children. It is available for purchase from the Child Witness to Violence Project (address listed above).

The Child Development-Community Policing Program, Yale Child Study Center, Yale University School of Medicine, 230 South Frontage Road, New Haven, CT 06520. This program brings police officers and mental health clinicians together for training and multidisciplinary intervention on behalf of children and families exposed to violence. It has a wealth of materials and experience. Contact the program at (203) 785-7947. Web site: http.info.med.yale.edu/chldstdy/cdcp.

Connelly, C. *Children Exposed to Violence: Criminal Justice Resources.* Washington, D.C.: National Criminal Justice Reference Service, 1999. This manual is available free online at www.ncjrs.org/puborder.

Resources for Mental Health Clinicians

Shelter from the Storm: Clinical Intervention with Young Children Affected by Domestic Violence: A Curriculum for Mental Health Clinicians, 2000. Developed by the Child Witness to Violence Project at Boston Medical Center. A 230-page curriculum for a thirteen-hour training for child mental health clinicians who work with families and young children affected by domestic violence. It is available for purchase from the Child Witness to Violence Project (address listed above).

James, B. *Treating Traumatized Children.* Lexington, Mass.: Lexington Books, 1989.

Osofsky, J., and E. Fenechel, eds. *Protecting Young Children in Violent Environments: Building Staff and Community Strengths.* Washington, D.C.: Zero to Three, 2000. Available for purchase from Zero to Three, 734 15th Street, N.W., Suite 1000, Washington, D.C. 20005; tel.:(800) 899-4301.

———. *Islands of Safety: Assessing and Treating Young Victims of Violence.* Washington, D.C.: Zero to Three, 1996. Available for purchase from Zero to Three (address and phone number above).

———. *Caring for Infants and Toddlers in a Violent Environment: Hurt, Healing, and Hope.* Washington, D.C.: Zero to Three, 1994. Available for purchase from Zero to Three (address and phone number above).

www.bcm.tmc.edu/cta: The Child Trauma Academy Web site,

mentioned above, has extensive information about treating traumatized children, with a special focus on the neurobiological aspects of trauma.

Resources for Pediatricians

American Academy of Pediatrics, Committee on Child Abuse and Neglect. "The Role of the Pediatrician in Recognizing and Intervening on Behalf of Abused Women." *Pediatrics* 101, no. 6 (June 1998): 1091.

The Family Violence Prevention Fund. *Identifying and Responding to Domestic Violence: Consensus Recommendations for Child and Adolescent Health.* San Francisco: Family Violence Prevention Fund, 2002. Available from The Family Violence Prevention Fund, 383 Rhode Island Avenue, Suite 304, San Francisco, CA 94103-8900. Web site: endabuse.org.

Books for Young Children

Davis, D. *Something Is Wrong at My House: A Book About Parents' Fighting.* Seattle, Wash.: Parenting Press, 1984.

Deaton, W. *I Saw It Happen.* Alameda, Calif.: Hunter House, Inc., 1998.

——. *Living with My Family.* Alameda, Calif.: Hunter House, Inc., 1991.

Hochban, T. *Hear My Roar: A Story of Family Violence.* Toronto: Annick Press, 1994.

Lee, I., and K. Sylvester. *When Mommy Got Hurt: A Story for Young Children about Domestic Violence.* Charlotte, N.C.: KIDSRIGHTS, 1996.

Minnesota Coalition for Battered Women. *A Kid's Workbook on Family Violence.* St. Paul, Minn.: Minnesota Coalition for Battered Women, 1987.

Paris, S. *Mommy and Daddy Are Fighting.* Seattle, Wash.: The Seal Press, 1985.
Rogers, F., and H. Sharapan. *I Do and I Don't.* Pittsburgh, Penn.: Family Communications, Inc., 1992.
Trotter, M. *A Safe Place.* Morton Grove, Ill.: Albert Whitman and Co., 1997.

Political Action/Advocacy Groups for Young Children

Children's Defense Fund (CDF). CDF provides a strong voice for all the children of America who cannot vote, lobby, or speak for themselves. They pay particular attention to the needs of poor and minority children and those with disabilities. Address: 25 E Street, N.W., Washington, DC 20001; tel.: (202) 628-8787. Web site: childrensdefensefund.org.

National Center for Children and Poverty (NCCP). NCCP uses demographic research and program and policy analyses to identify and promote strategies that reduce young child poverty and that improve the lives of poor young children. Address: The Joseph L. Mailman School of Public Health of Columbia University, 154 Haven Avenue, New York, NY 10032; tel.: (212) 304-7100. Web site: http://cpmcnet.columbia.edu/dept/nccp.

Zero to Three/The National Center for Infants, Toddlers, and Families. This organization provides information about and advocacy for very young children and their families. Its particular expertise is on the first three years of life. Its aim is to strengthen and support families, practitioners, and communities to promote the healthy development of babies and toddlers. Address: 734 15th Street, Suite 1000, Washington, DC 20005; tel.: (202) 638-1144. Web site: zerotothree.org.

KidsPac is a political action committee to help elect and reelect candidates to Congress who have a strong concern for children and families. Address: 80 Trowbridge Street, Cambridge, MA 02138; tel.: (617) 492-2229.

Web Sites for General Information

The National Center for Children Exposed to Violence: NCCEV.org. This Web site promotes public and professional awareness of the effects of violence on children and information about traumatization and successful approaches to intervention. It also provides links for training and technical assistance to communities around the country that are developing collaborative efforts to respond to children and families exposed to violence.

The Minnesota Center against Violence and Abuse Electronic Clearinghouse: mincava.umn.edu. MINCAVA supports research and education and offers access to violence-related resources. It contains extensive resources on the subjects of domestic violence, child abuse, and children's exposure to violence.

Uniteforkids.org. This Web site was developed by Tvisions and the Child Witness to Violence Project. It contains information about children's exposure to domestic violence, including an extensive library of resources, and information specific to children and domestic violence.

The National Child Traumatic Stress Network: nctsnet.org. A national network of mental health treatment centers from urban and rural areas that specialize in providing services to children and families affected by trauma. The Web site provides information about the effects of trauma on children, effective intervention and treatment, and policy issues.

ACKNOWLEDGMENTS

This book exists because of the wisdom, encouragement, and generosity of many friends, families, and colleagues—some of whom I will thank by name, others whom for ethical reasons I acknowledge anonymously in public. My first thanks goes to the Open Society Institute, which awarded me an individual project fellowship to write this book. In my application for the fellowship, I stated my strong desire to share what we had learned from our project, and also said I needed to have time away from the front lines to be able to reflect on our work before I began to write. The fellowship provided this gift of time. The respite was generously offered by the Harvard Children's Initiative, which gave me a home for the year, and by Julie Wilson, director of the Malcolm Weiner Center for Social Policy at the Kennedy School of Government at Harvard University, who offered me an affiliation with the university. I owe particular gratitude to Rick Weissbourd, who facilitated my relationship with the Children's Initiative and who provided early and consistent encouragement to write the book.

This book would not have been possible without the generosity and insight of the staff of the Child Witness to Violence Project at Boston Medical Center. While I am the person who put the words on paper, they reflect the collective experience of my colleagues: Amy Bamforth, Andrea Bernard, Jeanne Burkes, Dorcas Liriano, Carmen Norona, Liz Roberts, Angie Searcy, and Aimee Thompson. I owe the greatest thanks to Judy Hunt and Maxine Weinreb, the senior members of our staff who led the project while I wrote this book and who have encouraged and supported me at every step of this process.

I also thank colleagues and friends who voiced the conviction that this book would make a contribution—and who believed that I actually could write a book: Clare Dalton, Lois Kantor, Betsy Nadas Seamans, Elena Cohen, Ann Fleck Henderson, Janet Carter, and Peter Jaffe.

Every project benefits from support that is public and visible. I am grateful to several leaders who have used their influence to raise concern about the impact of violence on children. Barry Zuckerman, chief of pediatrics at Boston Medical Center and co-founder of the Child Witness to Violence Project, has been an important mentor since I began work at the hospital. He has consistently encouraged my work and has challenged me to grow along with the project. Bill Harris, founder of KidsPac, has supported the project from the beginning, provided consultation on this book, and has offered a strong voice of leadership in advocating for better services for children affected by violence. Former Massachusetts Attorney General Scott Harshbarger used the prestige of his office to raise public concern about violence and children and provided strong support to me in the initial stages of developing this book.

As I wrote this book, I consulted with experts and practitioners who readily gave me time, information, and perspective: Marilyn Augustyn, Cynthia Dickstein, Jeff Edleson, George Friday, Eric Holder, Anne Marie Hunter, Jane Knitzer, Bessel van der Kolk, Steven Parker, Susan Schechter, and Deborah Smolover. Their wisdom has become part of the book.

This book would not have evolved from the proposal stage without the vision and experience of Deanne Urmy, my editor at Beacon Press. She helped bridge the gap to a wider audience and gave insightful editorial suggestions for improving the manuscript. When she left Beacon Press, she left the project in the hands of Julie Hassel, who guided it to its completion.

Finally, my deepest gratitude goes to families: the families we have come to know in the Child Witness to Violence Project and my own family, which has nurtured and supported me at every step of this long process. The families of our project have taught me about courage, survival, and resilience. My children, Jeanie and Rebecca, helped me keep a balanced perspective about the project. My husband, Tim, and my sister Cynty functioned as the front-line editorial team, providing feedback on the many drafts of this book. Their enthusiasm and their willingness to support me with grace and humor have made this work possible.

INDEX